Swahili Made Easy

A BEGINNER'S COMPLETE COURSE

Swahili Made Easy

A BEGINNER'S COMPLETE COURSE

J.F. Safari

MKUKI NA NYOTA
DAR-ES-SALAAM

KIMECHAPISHWA NA
Mkuki Na Nyota Publishers Ltd
Nyerere Road, Quality Plaza Building
P. O. BOX. 4246, Dar es Salaam
publish@mkukinanyota.com
www. mkukinanyota.com

First Published by Tanzania Publishing House.

1972, 1987, 1992, 1996, 2002, 2005

ISBN 978-9987-08-503-3

CONTENTS

PART TWO

Lessons

KEY TO EXERCISES

VOCABULARY

DIBAJI

Kiswahili ni lugha ya Afrika Mashariki. Maendeleo ya lugha hii yamekuwa makubwa sana hata kuifanya iwe mojawapo ya lugha maarufu duniani. Licha ya kuwa lugha ya wananchi wa Afrika Mashariki, Kiswahili kinazungumzwa pia katika sehemu kadha za Afrika ya Kati.

Katika sehemu mbalimbali za ulimwengu, watu wengi wameingiwa na msisimko wa kujifunza lugha hii maarufu ya Afrika.

Kwa sababu hii "Waswahili" wenye uwezo wa kusaidia ufundishaji na ustawishaji wa Kiswahili nje ya eneo lao wanao wajibu mkubwa wa kutoa msaada huo.

Mmojawapo wa misaada muhimu itakiwayo sasa ni vitabu vya Kiswahili vya kuwasaidia wageni wapendao kujifunza lugha hii.

Ingawa viko vitabu vichache vilivyoandikwa kuhusu somo hili, ukweli ni kwamba vingi kati ya hivyo havitoshelezi wala kukidhi haja ya hivi sasa.

Kitabu hiki kilichoandikwa na Dr. Safari ni matokeo ya utafiti na majaribio ya muda mrefu. Majaribio ya kitabu hiki aliyafanya na vikundi mbalimbali vya wageni aliokuwa anawafundisha Kiswahili. Majaribio haya ameyafanya na vikundi vya Wajerumani wakati alipokuwa Ujerumani na wageni kutoka nchi zingine waliokuja kuitumikia Tanzania. Kutokana na utafiti na majaribio yake naweza kusema kuwa kitabu hiki kimetungwa kwa kufuata misingi ya utaalamu wa lugha.

Ingawa majaribio mengi yamefanywa kwa kutumia vikundi vya wageni, hii haina maana kuwa watu wengine hawawezi kufaidika na yaliyomo katika kitabu hiki. Ni matumaini yangu kuwa hata Watanzania na Waafrika wengine wenye ari ya kujifunza Kiswahili watanufaika na kazi hii.

Mwisho, natoa pongezi kwa mwandishi kwa juhudi yake hii na namwombea heri na ufanisi zaidi katika ujenzi, ustawishaji na uenezaji wa lugha hii ya Kiswahili.

G.A. Mhina

Aliyekuwa Mkurugenzi wa
Taasisi ya Uchunguzi wa Kiswahili
Chuo Kikuu cha Dar Es Salaam

INTRODUCTION

Africa has more languages than any other continent. Swahili is one of these languages. It belongs to a group called "Bantu". One of the characteristics of the Bantu languages is lack of articles and gender (masculine, feminine, neuter). The nouns in these tongues are grouped into "classes" by means of their nominal prefixes, e.g. *m*, *wa*, *ki*, and *vi*, as will become clearer in the course of this study.

The name "Swahili" is derived from the Arabic word *sawahel*, which means "coasts". Swahili is therefore the language of the people of the coast of East Africa. Although it contains a number of loan words, mostly from Arabic, Swahili is essentially an African language. In the nineteenth century, Bishop Steere of Zanzibar regarded Swahili as a key to the understanding of the culture of East Africa.

His remark was very much to the point, for by learning Swahili one learns at the same time the cultural values of the Swahili-speaking people.

Until now most of the books that are used by adult foreign students of Swahili were written in Europe or America by non-Swahili-speakers. Valuable as these books may be, they tend to be professional and too detailed, so much so that they discourage new learners. The author became aware of this fact when he was teaching "Swahili for Beginners" in the then West Germany (1970 - 73) and in Tanzania (1974 - to date).

This book is, therefore, a result of many years of teaching experience. The author has, with the help of his students (from all walks of life, and from different countries) written this book to meet a real need, the need of a foreign student who is coming in contact with Swahili for the first time.

While avoiding unnecessary details and linguistic technicalities, the book covers all the essential parts of speech of the Swahili language. The exercises have been carefully prepared and tested in class with various groups of students. They are designed to help the students learn correct Swahili by easy and rapid stages.

The book is in two parts. The first part consists of progressive lessons with test exercises. The second part is in form of a story about everyday events in the life of a Swahili family. At the end of each lesson there are comprehension and conversation exercises. It is taken for granted that the student is well prepared to follow Swahili as it is spoken. A certain amount of vocabulary is given at the beginning of each lesson. This, however, is not meant by any means, to be exhaustive. In case one does not understand the meaning of a word used in the text, reference should be made to the vocabulary and the translation provided at the end of the book. Useful phrases are another feature of the second part. They are provided for reference, and should be studied leisurely.

Nouns and verbs are listed in the appendix. The nouns are arranged according to their nominal prefixes, and the verbs are listed alphabetically by their stem forms. It is the sincere hope of the author and all those who helped him in this task that enough guidelines and exercises have been given to enable foreign students not only to acquire knowledge of written Swahili but also to develop a habit of speaking it fluently. Remember: "Practice makes perfect."

Attention is drawn to the fact that the Swahili-English and English-Swahili vocabulary contains only words used in the exercises. It follows therefore, that words in the lists of useful phrases should be learnt where and when they appear. The English-Swahili word list is very short due to the fact that exercises in English are few. The experience of the present writer and that of many who have taught Swahili to foreign students confirms the statement that: "Swahili is an easy language, its use is widespread, and it may be that there is no language easier to learn. There are no real difficulties of pronunciation, and none of spelling".

The writer, therefore, assures the foreign student of success once he/she begins seriously to learn this beautiful and useful African

Language. Although this manual has been especially prepared for use by foreign students, it will no doubt, be found useful also by Swahili-speaking students. General teaching experience proves that what is framed for a special group (in this case, the foreign student) is almost always found useful in the education of other groups as well.

This book lays no claim to being original, or possessing a magical key to easy learning, but it has one claim to make - it has been written by a SwahiIi-speaking author with the help of Swahili students from all over the world (East Africa, Japan, India, China, U.K., U.S.A., France, Italy, Brazil, Egypt, Algeria, Nigeria, Zambia, Ethiopia, Somalia, Burundi, Lesotho, Malawi, Sri Lanka, etc.) who joined the writer's course: "Swahili for Beginners."

In conclusion, the author would like to express his deep gratitude to all those who helped him to make this book a reality. Special thanks are due to Mr C. Kapinga for his valuable suggestions; to Mr G. Mhina for his encouragement and for writing a foreword to this edition, and last but not least to all his students, who are too many to mention individually by name.

J.F.S.

PART ONE

LESSON 1 - 28

LESSON 1

THE SWAHILI PRONUNCIATION

It is not difficult to pronounce Swahili if one observes the following rules:

All consonants, except G, have the same sounds as in English. The Swahili F is always pronounced as the English f in "*fit*" "*fair*" it is never pronounced as the f "of" which sounds like the Swahili v.

G is always hard, as in English, "go", "good".

S is always pronounced like the *s* in "soft," and never like the s in "visit".

Two consonants are sometimes used to produce one sound thus:

CH has the same sound as in English , "change", "check".

DH sounds like the *th* in "father", "feather".

SH has the same sound as the word, "shake".

TH sounds something like the sound in "thin", "think".

The sounds *dh* and *th* are Arabic and many good Swahili speakers find them difficult to pronounce. They often say *z* and *s* for *dh* and *th* respe ctively.

A few words give trouble even to Swahili-speakers. They are: *ghali,* "expensive", *ghafula,* "suddenly", *lugha,* "language", *gharama,* "expenses", etc. Some pronounce these words as if they were written with a hard *g* while others try to retain the Arabic guttural sound *gh.* Swahili has five vowels.

They are: a, e, i, o, u. Each vowel has only one sound.

a is always like the *a* in " father";

e.g. baba, "*father*".

e is always like the e in "weigh";

e. g. *wewe*, " you".

i is always like the ee in "see";

e.g. *sisi*, "we".

o is always like the aw in "law";

e.g. *soko*, "market ".

u is always like the oo in "cook";

e.g. *kuku*, "hen".

The vowels are sometimes used together like this: *saa*, "watch, hour"; taa, "lamp" etc. Each vowel must be pronounced distinctly because they belong to different words; e.g. *kufa*, "to die", is distinguished from *kufaa* "to be useful," by the doubling of the final *a.* So, too, *kukata,* "to cut", and *kukataa* "to refuse"; *kuku,* "hen", and *kukuu*, "old, ancient". These words are further distinguished by the accent which falls on different syllables according to the rule given below.

The Swahili accent is constant and falls on the second to last syllable: e.g. *Kitabu*, "book", *Kiswahili,* etc. There is only one exception to this rule, the word *barabara,* "exactly", which has the accent on the third from last syllable. This distinguishes it from another word with the same spelling: *baraba'ra*, "road" which has the usual accent on the second from last syllable.

LESSON 2

SWAHILI GREETINGS AND MANNERS

Jambo is the commonest form of greeting used in East Africa. It is used from morning till evening to greet friends, relatives, visitors and strangers. It is a corruption of *Hujambo*? "How are you?" and *Sijambo* "I am well". It also means "Hello", "good morning", "good day", etc.

The answer to *Jambo* is *Jambo*, and to *Hujambo*? is *Sijambo*. *Habari gani*? "what is the news?" "How are you?" is also used after *Jambo*, or even instead of it. Swahili-speaking people, like all other Africans, have a long litany of greetings as follows:

Amina Hujambo, Tatu?

Tatu Sijambo, habari gani?

Amina Nzuri tu, habari za nyumbani?

Tatu Nzuri, habari za watoto?

Amina Nzuri, habari za bibi na shangazi?

Tatu Nzuri.

The meaning of the above greetings is as follows: Amina starts by saying *Hujambo*? "How are you?" and Tatu says *Sijambo*, "I am well", and then they ask each other about their relatives at home, and each answers, as usual, *Nzuri.* "well". Social change, especially in towns, is affecting this custom.

Many people cut short the greetings because of work, and other duties.

Hodi is another form of greeting. It is used by visitors (before they enter the house) to announce their arrival to their hosts inside the house. It is not used in the streets except when one wants to push one's way through a crowd. *Hodi* may be compared to the European custom of knocking at the door. As Swahili doors are always open when people are around, it was necessary to invent a way of announcing one's arrival to the inmates of a house.

The answer to *hodi* is *karibu,* "you are welcome." To make sure that you are really welcome to the house, wait for another *karibu* or *karibu ndani* "come in". If there are two or more visitors, the answer will be *karibuni.* While inside the house, you may hear: *Karibu kiti*, "Won't you sit down?" To which you answer, *Asante.* "Thank you." Some people say *starehe,* "I am comfortable", instead of *asante.* You are free to use either form.

You may also be told *Karibu chai*, "Welcome to a cup of tea". It is good manners not to refuse to partake of anything offered. Total refusal may be regarded as an insult, especially if you belong to a different ethnic group or social class. Take a little as a token of good will and appreciation of their hospitality.

Shikamoo is yet another form of greeting which is widely used to greet those higher in social status or older in age. The answer is *marahaba.* No English equivalent is known to the author. It is a greeting as well as an expression of respect due to old men/women and rulers in the traditional Swahili communities.

When greeting a person who is afflicted by some disaster, such as death of a near relative, disease or loss of property, say *pole* "sorry," "take it easy", after *jambo* or *habari gani*? The answer to *pole* is *asante*, "thank you", or *nimekwisha poa*, "that's how things are with me." Don't confuse it with *polepole,* "slowly". After greeting people, we sometimes wish to congratulate them on any happy event, e.g.

marriage, birth of a child, etc., so we say, *hongera,* "congratulations". The answer to *hongera* is *asante.*

When leaving you say: *Kwa heri,* "good bye". If you are taking leave of more than one person say: *Kwa herini.* "good bye". The answer to *kwa heri* is *kwa heri.* If two or more persons are leaving, you say to them: *Kwa herini,* "good bye", or "may you fare well." Some people like to say: *Tutaonana,* "I will be seeing you again." Literally, however, the phrase means: "we shall meet", or "we shall see each other again." Many Swahili speakers say *tutaonana* after *kwa heri,* while some simply say *tutaonana* instead of *kwa heri.* Yet others say *kwa heri ya kuonana,* "good bye, see you again".

EXERCISE 1

1. What is the answer to *Hodi*?
2. What is the answer to *Hujambo*?
3. What is the answer to *Habari gani*?
4. What does *Karibu kiti* mean? How do you respond?
5. When is *Shikamoo* used and what is the answer to it?
6. What is the plural of *Karibu?*
7. When leaving what do you say?
8. What do you say when pushing your way through a crowd?
9. What do you say to someone afflicted or hurt?
10. What is the answer to *Pole?*
11. How would you congratulate someone in Swahili?
12. What is the answer to *Hongera?*

LESSON 3

THE CLASSIFICATION OF SWAHILI NOUNS

Swahili is one of the African languages known as Bantu. One of the characteristics of these languages is the division of nouns into classes, and not into masculine, feminine and neuter genders. The noun classes are distinguished by their nominal prefixes. Swahili nouns, therefore, consist of a root of the word and a prefix, as follows:

From the stem *-tu,* and the prefix *m* we get *mtu,* "a person", "a human being". Likewise, from the root *tu* and the prefix *ki* we get *kitu,* "a thing", "something". The plurals of these two words are formed from the same root with the prefixes *wa* and *vi* respectively; thus: *watu,* "people"; *vitu* "things".

For the sake of classification we count *mtu, watu,* as one class, and *kitu, vitu* as another class. In the following pages we are going to deal with each class separately. There are eight classes but most of the nouns are found in the first five classes, as will be seen below.

THE M-WA CLASS

In this class the nouns begin with *m* in the singular and *wa* in the plural. They usually denote human beings. They are:

Mtu, man, person	*watu,* people, persons
mke, wife	*wake,* wives
mume, husband	*waume,* husbands
mgeni, guest, stranger	*wageni,* guests, strangers

mtoto, child	*watoto,* children
mpishi, cook	*wapishi,* cooks
mganga, doctor	*waganga,* doctors
mzee[11], old man	*wazee,* old men
mgonjwa, sick person	*wagonjwa,* sick persons
mlevi, drunkard	*walevi,* drunkards
mkulima, farmer	*wakulima*, farmers
mkurugenzi, director	*wakurugenzi,* directors
mvulana, boy	*wavulana,* boys
msichana, girl	*wasichana*, girls
Mzungu, European	*Wazungu*, Europeans
Mhindi, Indian	*Wahindi*, Indians
mtumishi, servant	*watumishi*, servants

Two nouns which do not denote human beings are:

mdudu, insect	*wadudu*, insects
mnyama, animal	*wanyama*, animals

Whenever the root of a noun belonging to this class begins with a vowel, *w* is inserted between the root and the prefix *m*, e.g. - *alimu* becomes *mwalimu; - ana* becomes *mwana,* etc.

The following are among the commonest nouns of this kind:

mwalimu, teacher	*walimu,* teachers
mwanamke, woman	*wanawake*, women
mwanamume, man	*wanaume*, men
mwana, one's own child	*wana,* one's own children
mwanadamu, human being	*wanadamu,* human beings

1 *mzee* is not only an old man, but also a wise, honourable man.

mwanafunzi, student	*wanafunzi*, students
mwenzi, companion	*wenzi,* companions
mwenyewe, oneself	*wenyewe,* themselves
mwenyeji, inhabitant	*wenyeji*. (inhabitants inatives, local persons)
mwizi/mwivi, thief	*wezi (wevi)*[2], thieves
mwongo, liar	*waongo*, liars

EXERCISE 2

Translate the following words into English:

1. Wanafunzi, wezi, wanawake, wenzi, mgeni, mtumishi.
2. Mlevi, mke, mume, mkurugenzi, mpishi, mzee, mwongo.
3. Mtu, mwana, mgonjwa, msichana, mvulana, mtoto, mwizi.

Change into the plural:

4. Mwongo, mwizi, mwenzi, mwanamke, mwanamume, mume, mwalimu.
5. Msichana, mwanadamu, mzee, mwanafunzi, mtoto, mgeni.

The following nouns denote human relationships:

baba, father	*baba,* fathers
mama, mother	*mama,* mothers
dada, sister	*dada,* sisters
babu, grandfather	*mababu,* grandfathers

2 *wezi* and *wevi,* are formed from *waizi* and *waivi.* In cases like this one the *ai* changes into *e.*

bibi[3], grandmother	*bibi,* grandmothers
shangazi, aunt	*shangazi,* aunts
rafiki[4], friend	*marafiki,* friends
adui, enemy	*maadui,* enemies
ndugu, relative	*ndugu,* relatives
kaka, elder brother	*kaka,* elder brothers
bwana, master	*bwana*[5], masters

The following nouns denote disabled persons:

Kipofu[6], a blind person	*vipofu,* blind persons
kiziwi, a deaf person	*viziwi,* deaf persons
kiwete, a lame person	*viwete,* lame persons

Two nouns beginning with *ki-* **which show no disability are:**

kijana, a young person	*vijana*, young persons
kiongozi, a leader	*viongozi,* leaders

3 *bibi,* means also lady, and has *mabibi* for plural.

4 marafiki is often heard as the plural of rafiki.

5 *mabwana* is also used to mean masters, lords.

6 The prefix ki (plural vi) is usually used for things. It is beyond the scope of this work to grapple with the ethnolinguistic problem as to why the Swahili use these prefixes to denote disabled persons. This is something you can discuss with your teacher.

LESSON 4

THE SWAHILI ADJECTIVE

In Swahili the adjectives agree with the nouns they qualify both in number and in nominal prefixes. With the exception of *kila* "each", "every", all adjectives follow their nouns.

e.g. *kila mtoto,* "every child", but

mtoto mdogo, "a small child".

The following is a list of Swahili adjectives. It is not exhaustive. It contains, however, most of the commonly used adjectives. Note that those which are preceded by a dash, take the nominal prefixes, and those which are not preceded by a dash do not take any prefix:

__ *dogo,* small, little	__ *gumu* hard, difficult
__ *kubwa,* big, great	__ *zima,* whole, living
__ *refu*, long, high	__ *pya*, new
__ f*upi*, short, shallow	__ *chungu,*bitter, sour
__ *zuri,* nice, pretty	__ *tamu*, sweet
__ *baya*, bad, ugly	__ *chache,* few
__ *kali*, sharp, fierce	__ *nene,* fat
__ *pole,* mild, gentle	__ *nono,* fat (animal)
__ *kavu,* dry	__ *chafu,* dirty
__ *bichi,* unripe, raw	__ *vivu,* lazy

__ *bovu*, rotten, broken	__ *kuu,* great
__ *pana,* wide	__ *tupu*, empty
__ *embamba,* slender	__ *ote,* all, whole
__ *zito,* heavy	__ *epesi* light, easy
__ *ema*, kind, good	__ *erevu,* cunning
__ *ekundu,* red	__ *ingi,* much, many
__ *eusi,* black	__ *ingine*, other
__ *eupe,* white	

The following adjectives do not take nominal prefixes:

bora, excellent	*safi,* clean
hafifu, poor (quality)	*rasmi,* official
hodari, brave, skilful	*halisi* genuine
ghali, expensive	*rahisi,* cheap, easy
haba, few, rare	*imara,* firm, strong
kamili, complete, exactly, on the dot	*laini,* soft
tajiri rich	*maskini* poor
tele, abundant	

Here are some examples of adjectives agreeing with their nouns:

Singular		Plural
mtoto mdogo,	a small child	*watoto wadogo*
mwalimu hodari,	a good teacher	*walimu hodari*
kitabu cheusi,	a black book	*vitabu vyeusi*

mtu mwerevu[7],	a cunning man	*watu werevu*
mwizi mkubwa,	a big thief	*wezi wakubwa*
uso mweupe,	a white face	*nyuso nyeupe*
lugha rahisi,	an easy language	*lugha rahisi*

EXERCISE 3

Add the right prefixes to each of the following adjectives (in brackets):

1. Mgeni (safi)
2. Watu (ekundu)
3. Walevi (ingi)
4. Wapishi (hodari)
5. Wagonjwa (chache)
6. Watoto (eusi)
7. Mwalinu (eupe)
8. Mke(ema)
9. Wanaume (hodari)
10. Watu (ote)
11. Baba (kali)
12. Wake (hodari)
13. Wanaume (zito)
14. Watoto (fupi)
15. Wazee (refu)
16. Mgonjwa (epesi)
17. Mwanamke (bora)
18. Wanafunzi (ingi)
19. Mpishi (zuri)
20. Watoto (-dogo)

7 The plural of adjectives beginning with *e* is *we* in the *mw* class, *vye* in the *ki/vi; mye* in *m/mi, me* in *ma; nye* in *N*; in *pee* in pg. For the plural of U class see *N*, i.e. *nye*. Likewise *ote* - has *wote, vyote* etc. e.g. *watu wote,* "all people", *vitu vyote,* "all things", *pahali pote,* all places", *miti yote,* "all trees", *nyumba zote,* "all houses" etc.

EXERCISE 4

Using the word *ni* to translate "is" and "are", change the following into the plural forms:

1. Mpishi ni mganga hodari na kipofu ni mtu mzuri.
2. Mgeni ni mwanamke mzuri na ni mke hodari.
3. Mzee ni mlevi mkubwa na msichana ni mwanamke mdogo.
4. Mwizi ni mwerevu na ni mtu mwongo na mbaya.
5. Mwalimu ni mtu mwema na ni baba mzuri.
6. Mtumishi ni mtu mfupi na mwerevu.

EXERCISE 5

Translate into Swahili:

1. Mothers are good cooks; doctors are good people.
2. Men and women are people; children are small people.
3. Servants are nice men; servants are women.
4. The visitors are tall men; the visitors are white men.
5. Tatu is a good wife and Mashaka is a good child.
6. Many men are good husbands and many women are good wives.
7. Many pupils are small children and many teachers are old men.
8. Many people are sick, few men are doctors.
9. Many guests are tall people, few are short.
10. Amina is an excellent teacher and a very good mother.
11. Blind men are few; blind women are many.
12. The children are all white and the old men are all black.

LESSON 5

THE MI - MI CLASS

In this class we find names of trees, members of the human body, household articles, and some physical phenomena. Examples:

Singular	Plural
mti, tree	*miti*, trees
mkono, hand, arm	*mikono*, hands, arms
mguu, leg, foot	*miguu*, legs, feet
mgongo, back	*migongo*, backs
mdomo, mouth, lip	*midomo*, mouths, lips
mwili, body	*miili*, bodies
moyo, heart	*mioyo* hearts
moto, fire	*mioto*, fires
moshi, smoke	*mioshi*, smokes
mto, 1. river 2. pillow	*mito*, 1. rivers 2. *mito* pillows
mji, town, city	*miji* towns,cities
mkate, bread	*mikate*, bread (loaves of)
mstari, line	*mistari*, lines
mtende, palm tree	*mitende*, palm trees
mwaka, year	*miaka*, years
mwezi, moon, month	*miezi*,months,
mwanzo, beginning	*mianzo*, beginnings
mwisho, end	*miisho*, ends

The adjectives which qualify these nouns take *m* and *mi,* thus: *mti; mrefu.* "a tall tree ", *miti mirefu,* "tall trees"; *mwanzo mzuri,* "a good beginning", *(pl) mianzo mizuri,* "good beginnings"

Using *ni* for is and are, we have: *Mtende ni mti mrefu.* "A palm tree is a tall tree." Nairobi *ni mji mkubwa,* "Nairobi is a big city." *Mwanzo mzuri na mwisho mbaya,* "A good beginning and a bad end".

Using *ana* for "he, she, has", and *wana*[8] for "they have" translate the following into Swahili (e.g. for No.1 the translation is: *Mtoto mdogo ana mikono na miguu midogo.)*[9]

EXERCISE 6

1. A small child has small hands and small legs.
2. Short men have short legs, and tall men have long legs.
3. She has a good heart and nice lips.
4. The beginning is difficult but the end is easy.
5. Teachers and doctors have kind hearts.
6. Patients are many but doctors are few.
7. Palm trees are very tall and have long roots
8. Light hearts are good but heavy hearts are also good.
9. Mashaka has long legs and a big mouth.
10. Long years are many but short years are few.

---

8 *Ana* means "he / she has", but it is used even when the subject precedes it; e.g. *Ana* mtoto mdogo, "he/she has a small child". So too Tatu ana mtoto mdogo, "Tatu has a small child". Likewise.

wana, "they have": *Wana watoto wengi,* "they have many children". Again, *Wanawake wana watoto wengi.* "Women have many children"

9 *Lakini* but

LESSON 6

THE KI-VI CLASS

Nouns in this class denote things. There are a few nouns which denote living things (*see Lesson Three*).

Here are the commonest nouns in this class:

kitu, thing	*vitu,* things
kiti, chair	*viti,* chairs
kitabu, book	*vitabu,* books
kisu, knife	*visu,* knives
kitanda, bed	*vitanda,* beds
kikombe, cup	*vikombe,* cups
kikapu, basket	*vikapu,* baskets
kichwa, head	*vichwa,* heads
kiatu, shoe	*viatu,* shoes
kiazi, potato	v*iazi,* potatoes
kifua, chest	*vifua,* chests
kidole, finger	*vidole,* fingers
kijiko, spoon	*vijiko,* spoons
kisima, well	*visima,* wells
kisiwa, island	*visiwa,* islands

The adjectives agreeing with this class have *ki/vi* prefixes, e.g. *kitabu kizuri,* "a nice book"; *vitabu vizuri,* "nice books".

EXERCISE 7

Translate into Swahili:

1. Long fingers.
2. He has a big head.
5. Very nice shoes
6. Thieves have broad chests.

3. She has a long bed.
4. Many potatoes.
7. Sharp Knives
8. A big basket

Some nouns in this class begin with *ch* and *vy*, e.g.

chakula, food — *vyakula,* foods
cheti, certificate — *vyeti,* certificates
cheo, rank, measure — *vyeo,* ranks, measures
choo, toilet — *vyoo,* toilets
chombo, vessel — *vyombo*, vessels
chuma iron — *vyuma*, pieces of iron
chumba, room — *vyumba,* rooms

Adjectives also begin with *ch* and *vy* if the stems begin with a vowel, e.g. -eusi: *kiatu cheusi* "a black shoe"; *viatu vyeusi* "black shoes". Likewise, a light basket" *kikapu chepesi.* "Light baskets" *vikapu vyepesi.*

EXERCISE 8

Add the correct nominal prefixes to the following adjectives (in brackets):

1. vitabu (eusi)
2. viti (epesi)
3. chumba (eupe)
4. kikombe (dogo)
5. chuma (laini)
6. chombo (embamba)
7. mtoto ana viazi (eupe)
8. watoto wana viazi (eupe)
9. chakula (dogo)
10. vyakula (dogo)
11. vitu (ingi)
12. vyuma (kubwa)
13. viti (refu)
14. visu (kali)
15. viazi (ghali)
16. viazi (rahisi)
17. kikombe (dogo)

LESSON 7

THE N CLASS

Although this class is known as the *N* class, not every noun in this class begins with an *N*. The nouns in this class, however, have one thing in common; they retain the same form for both singular and plural, as will be shown below:

Nouns that begin with *N*:

ndege, bird(s); aircraft
ndizi, banana(s)
ngoma, drum(s)
ng'ombe, cow, cattle
ngurumo, thunder(s)
nguvu, strength (s)
nguo, cloth, clothes
nyoka, snake(s)
nyumba, house(s)
nyuki, bee(s)
njaa, hunger, famine
njia, way(s)
njugu, peanut(s)
nzige, locust(s)
nyama meat

Some nouns which have *b* and *v* in the root, change *N* into *M,* thus: *nb* becomes *mb*, as in: *mbwa,* "a dog, dogs"; *mbu* "mosquito(s)"; *mbegu* "seed(s)"; *mboga* "vegetable(s)"; *nv* becomes *mv*, as in: *mvua* "rain(s)"; *mvi* 'gray hair(s)'; *mvinyo* "wine, spirits".

The following nouns belong to the *N* class altbough they do not begin with *N*:

barua, letter(s)
bahasha, envelope(s)
barabara, road(s)
mvua, rain
sukari, sugar
ardhi, earth, land

chumvi, salt	*asali,* honey
chupa, bottle(s)	*asubuhi*, morning
faida, profit	*anga*, sky
hasara, loss	*habari,* news
fedha, money	*hatari,* danger
furaha, joy	*hesabu*, sums, arithmetic
huzuni, sadness	*meza,* table (s)
kalamu, pencil(s)	*saa,* hour(s), watch(es)
lugha, language	*taa*, lamp(s)
nazi coconut(s)	*siku,* day (s)

Adjectives qualifying nouns of the *N* class take the *N* prefix or both singular and plural, e.g. *nyumba nzuri,* "nice house(s)"; *ndizi ndogo*, "small banana(s)".

1. Adjectives which begin with *ch, f, k, p, t*, take no prefix:

e.g.	*ndizi chache,*	a few bananas
	njia fupi,	a short way
	nyumba kubwa,	big house(s)
	njia pana,	*wide,* broad way(s)
	ndizi tamu,	sweet banana(s)

2. *N* before b, like *baya*, and *-pya*, becomes *m*, e.g. *njaa mbaya* bad famine", *nyumba mpya*, new bouse(s)

3. For *nj, nd* is used, thus: *njia ndefu* a long way·. (Some people still say *njia refu,* but this is not accepted in standard Swahili.)

USEFUL PHRASES

habari gani?	what is the news? how are you?
saa ngapi?	what is the time?
hatari mbele,	danger ahead
polepole,	slowly
chai tayari,	tea is ready
chai ya rangi,	tea without milk
kahawa ya rangi,	coffee without milk
weka chai mezani	put tea on the table
karibu chai, ndugu	welcome to a cup of tea, brother

EXERCISE 9

Translate into Swahili:

1. sweet coconuts
2. big tables
3. a long hour
4. profit and loss
5. joy and sadness
6. tea and sugar
7. bread and meat
8. potatoes and salt
9. much money
10. a broad way
11. a few hours
12. a sharp pencil
13. good news or bad news
14. a light bottle
15. long hours

LESSON 8

THE MA CLASS

This class has been named after its plural prefix *ma*. It has no singular prefix, or as some say, it lost it in the process of transformation common to all living languages. The singular prefix however, reappears in the verbs and possessive adjectives (*langu, lako. lenu,* etc,) as will become clear after we have dealt with verbs and adjectives.

Here are some of the commonest nouns in this class:

jambo, matter	*mambo*, matters
jina, name	*majina,* names
jino, tooth	*meno*, teeth
jicho, eye	*macho*, eyes
*jibu, a*nswer	*majibu,* answers
jiko, kitchen	*meko,* kitcchen
jiwe, stone	*mawe,* stones
sikio, ear	*masikio,* ears
swali, question	*maswali,* questions
tunda, fruit	*matunda*, fruits
shamba, field, farm	*mashamba,* fields, farms
samduku, box suitcase	*masanduku*, boxes, suitcases

The following nouns are used only in their plural form:

mafuta, oil	*matata,* trouble
maji, water	*mahindi,* maize
maziwa, milk	*mazungumzo*, talk, conversation
maradhi, diseases	*mate,* saliva
majani, grass	*maajabu*, wonders

Adjectives remain unchanged in the singular, and have *ma* prefix in the plural. Thus:

jina zuri, a good name
swali gumu, a difficult question
majina mazuri, good names
maswali magumu, difficult questions

EXERCISE 10

Translate into Swahili:

1. The child has nice eyes and big ears.
2. Teachers have sharp eyes and wide ears.
3. The dog has a nice name.
4. The question is difficult but the answer is easy.
5. Old men discuss *(jadili)* important *(muhimu)* matters.
6. The women with big boxes have good news.
7. Small children have water, mothers have milk.
8. Bananas and fruits; houses and doors; fields and grass.
9. Big stones are few but small are mamy
10. Eyes and ears are wonders; rain and rivers also.

EXERCISE 11

Add the right prefixes:

1. Watoto wana mikono -dogo na macho - kubwa.
2. Wageni ni -ingi na -ote ni watu -zuri.
3. Viti ni -chache na watoto ni -engi.
4. Ndizi ni matunda -tamu na ni -ingi.
5. Mikate ni -zuri na ni -ingi.
6. Chakula ni -ghali lakini ni -dogo.
7. Kiswahili ni lugha -zuri na -rahisi.
8. Nyumba ni -kubwa lakini vyumba ni -dogo.
9. Milango ni -pana na -zuri lakini -chache.
10. Wagonjwa ni watu -pole na walimu ni watu -bora.

LESSON 9

THE U CLASS

The nouns in this class begin with *u* (or *w* before a vowel) in the singular. Most of them have no plural, and those that do have taken the plural formed of the *N* class. Many of these nouns are derivative, i.e. they are formed by simply prefixing *u* to the stems of other nouns and adjectives. e.g. From *moja*, "one", we get *umoja*, "unity"; from -*zuri*, "beautiful" we get *uzuri*, "beauty".

1. Here are some more nouns formed from other nouns and adjectives:

uzuri, beauty,	*ukubwa*, greatness, size
urefu, length, height, depth	*udogo*, smallness
ufupi, brevity, shortness	*uzee*, old age
utu, humanity	*utoto*, childhood
utumwa, slavery	*ubaba*, fatherhood
wizi, theft	*ujanja*, cleverness

2. The following are collective nouns:

unga, flour,	*wali*, cooked rice
udongo, earth, soil	*ugali* stiff porridge *ugali*
uji, gruel	*ushanga*, beads(s)
utitiri crowd (of fleas)	*ufuta*, oil-seed, sesame seed/oil simsim

3. The following nouns, like those in sections 1 and 2, have no plurals:

usiku, night, at night	*usingizi,* sleep
umri, age	*umeme,* electricity
ulimwengu, universe	*wino, ink*

4. Some nouns have the prefix *ma* in the plural, e.g.

ugonjwa, disease	*magonjwa,*diseases
ua, flower,	*maua*, flowers
ugomvi, quarrel,	*magonvi,* quarrels

5. The following nouns also have plurals:

a)	*ubao*, timber	*mbao*, timbers
	udevu, beard	*ndevu*, beard
	wimbo, song	*nyimbo,* songs
	uso, face	*nyuso* face
	ubavu, rib	*mbavu*, ribs
	wavu, net	*nyavu*.nets
b)	*ukuta,* wall	*kuta,*walls
	upepo, wind	*pepo,* winds
	ufagio, broom	*fagio,* brooms

Adjectives which qualify nouns of this class have the *m* prefix the singular and *n* in the plural; e.g.

uso mzuri, "a nice face"	*nyuso nzuri.* "nice faces"
wimbo mzuri "a nice song"	*nyimbo nzuri* "nice songs"
ujana ni mzuri ,"youth is good"	No plural

ukubwa ni kitu kizuri, "greatness is a good thing"	No plural
umoja ni nguvu, "unity is strength"	No plural

EXERCISE 12

Translate into Swahili:

1. Unity is strength; unity is a good thing.
2. Theft is bad, humanity is excellent
3. Songs are long but sweet.
4. Walls are high and wide.
5. Sleep is good at night.
6. Great age is very good but youth is excellent.
7. Diseases are bad.
8. The universe is big and wide.
9. The flour is good but the loaves of bread are bad.
10. The flowers in the garden (bustani) are beautiful.

LESSON 10

THE PA AND KU CLASSES

These two classess can be treated together, for they are simple and short. The *PA* class has only one word, *pahali* "a place" or "places". This word is sometimes replaced by *mahali,* whose meaning is the same. Adjectives qualifying this noun take the *pa* prefix, e.g. *pahali (mahali) pazuri,* "a good place, good places". *Mahali pabaya*, bad place, bad places."

The *KU* class contains all the verbs serving as nouns. As we shall see shortly, Swahili infinitives (nouns derived from verbs) begin with *KU*, e. g. *kusoma*, "to read, or reading".

The adjectives also take the *KU* prefix. Thus: *Kusoma ni kuzuri,* "reading is good". *Kuimba kwingi ni kubaya*, "Much singing is bad". *Kula sana ni kubaya,* "Too much eating is bad".

EXERCISE 13

Translate into Swahili:

1. Reading is good but too much reading is bad.
2. Big hotels have many rooms and nice beds.
3. Arusha is a big place; it has many people. At night there is nice singing and dancing (*kucheza dansi*)
4. The world is a beautiful place.
5. Walls are hard.
6. Eating bananas only (*tu)* is a bad habit (*tabia*).

NB More verbs will be given later on. You may use any of them as a noun following the rules given above.

LESSON 11

SWAHILI NUMBERS

Numbers one to five take nominal prefixes the rest do not.

1. moja, *mtu mmoja,* "one man", *kitabu kimoja.* "one book".
2. mbili (-wili) *watu wawili,* "two men"; vitabu viwili, "two books".
3. tatu *watu watatu,* "three men"; *viti vitatu* "three chairs".
4. nne, *watu wanne,* "four men," *viti vinne.*" four chairs·.
5. tano, *watu watano,* "five men; *viti vitano,* "five chairs".
6. sita, *watu sita.* "six men"; no prefix up to ten.
7. saba,
8. nane,
9. tisa,
10. kumi,
11. kumi na moja,
12. kumi na mbili. n.k.....
20. ishirini,
21. ishirini na moja
22. ishirini na mbili. n.k......
30. thelathini.
31. thelathini na moja.
32. thelathini na mbili. n.k......

40. arobaini,
41. arobaini na moja,
42. arobaini na mbili. n.k......
50. hamsini,
51. hamsini na rnoja,
52. hamsini na mbili, n.k......
60. sitini,
61. sitini na moja,
62. sitini na mbili, n.k......
70. sabini,
71. sabini na moja,
72. sabini na mbili, n.k......
80. themanini,
81. themanini na moja,
82. themanini na mbili, n.k....
90. tisini,
91. tisini na moja,
92. tisini na mbili, n.k.....
100. mia moja,
101. mia moja na moja,
102. mia moja na mbili, n.k...
110. mia moja na kumi,
111. mia moja na kumi na moja, n.k......
1,000. elfu moja au alfu moja,
1,001. elfu moja na moja,
1,010. elfu moja na kumi, n.k......
10,000. elfu kumi,
100,000. mia moja elfu au laki moja,
1,000,000. milioni moja.

HOW MUCH AND HOW OFTEN

mara moja, once, at once	e.g. *mbili mara mbili* (2 x 2)
mara mbili, twice	e.g. *tatu mara sita* (3 x 6)
mara sita, six times	
mara saba, seven times	
-ngapi? how many?	e.g. *watu wangapi?* How many people?" *vitabu vingapi?,* How many books
kiasi gani? how much?	e.g. *sukari kiasi gani?* "how much sugar?"
asilimia, percent, percentage	
kutoa, to subtract, minus	e.g. *kumi toa saba (10-7)*
kujumlisha to add	e.g. *tano jumlisha na tatu* (5+ 3)
kuzidisha, to multiply,	*saba zidisha na saba* (7 x 7)
kugawanya, to divide	*sita gawanya kwa mbili* (6÷2)
kufanya hesabu, to count things, to do arithmetic	
jumla, total	

EXERCISE 14

Answer in words:

1. Je, watu wangapi walifika hapa jana? (say 5)
2. Je, viti vingapi ni vibovu? (say 3)
3. Je, hamsini kutoa ishirini na moja ni ngapi? (50 - 21 =....)
4. Gawanya thelathini kwa tano (30÷5 =...)
5. Write in words: 10,000; 555; 432; 1678.
6. Write and answer in words: 10 x 15 ni 150.
7. 21 + 60 ni 81.
8. 907 - 678 ni ngapi?

LESSON 12

COMPARISON

In Swahili, adjectives do not change in order to express degrees of comparison. Swahili expresses equality and inequality by using the following words.

1. To express equality (or positive degree) *sawa na* "equal to " or *kama* "as...as", are used; e.g. *Tatu ni mrefu kama wewe,* "Tatu is as tall as you." *Kusoma ni kugumu sawa na kulima*, Reading is as hard as cultivating".

2. To denote inequality *kuliko* or *zaidi ya,* "more than" are used, e.g. *Tatu ni mzuri kuliko Pendo,* "Tatu is prettier than Pendo". *Tatu ni mwema zaidi ya Pendo. "Tatu is kinder than Pendo".*

3. To express the highest degree (superlative) *-ote,* is used after the words *kuliko* or *zaidi ya,* e.g.
   a. *Babu ni mzee kuliko wote,* "Grandfather is the oldest of all".
   b. *Ana kitabu kizuri kuliko vyote,* "He has the nicest book".
   c. *Ana akili zaidi ya watoto wote* "She is the most intelligent child".

As you may have noticed, *-ote,* "all " , agrees with the nouns being compared and takes their nominal prefixes. Compare a) and b) above and you will see that -ote takes the plural prefixes.

EXERCISE 15

Translate into Swahili:

1. Tatu is the nicest girl here but she is not the tallest.
2. Mashaka is as big as you, but he is shorter than you.
3. Kilimanjaro is the highest mountain in[10] Africa.
4. Tanzania is bigger than Kenya, but Nairobi is bigger than Dar es Salaam.
5. Is New York the largest city in the world[11] ?
6. Learning is better than swimming (use the adjective *bora*)[12]

---

10 "in" is usually not translated when referring to the towns, countries and places.

11 "in the world" – duniani

12 Other forms of expressing degrees of comparisons include the verbs: kupita "to surpass, kuzidi " to excel "kushinda" to beat"

LESSON 13

THE SWAHILI VERBS

In the infinitive, all Swahili verbs, as we have already said, begin with Ku (i.e. they add the prefix *ku* to the stem) which correspond, to the English word " to in "to go, to come, etc..." Here are some of the commonest verbs:

kusoma, to read, study	*kuona*, to see
kuandika, to write	*kulala*, to sleep, to lie down
kupika, to cook	*kuamka*, to wake up, to get up
kula, to eat	*kuenda*, (kwenda), to go
kunywa,to drink	*kuja*, to come
kuwa, to be	*kurudi*, to come back
kufika, to arrive	*kurudisha*, to give back
kuondoka, to depart	*kurudia*, to repeat
kujua, to know	*kufunga*, to shut, close up
kutaka, to want, wish	*kufungua*, to open
kuelewa, to understand	*kupenda*, to like, to love,
kuchoka, to be tired	*kucheka*,to laugh
kuvaa, to put on a dress, wear	*kuchuma*, to pick (flowers,etc.)
kufanya, to do	*kujifunza*, to learn, study
kufundisha, to teach	

Swahili verbs have four tenses designated by what may be called "tense markers", namely:

na, designates the present tense
me, expresses the perfect tense
li, designates the past tense
ta, designates the future tense.

This is the way tenses are expressed in the affirmative, as for the negative (*tenses see Lesson 17*).

A sentence contains a subject and a predicate. If the subject is a person, the following personal pronouns are used:

ni-,	*I*	*tu-*	*we*
u-,	*you (sing)*	*m-*	*you*
a-,	*he, she*	*wa-*	*they*

To make a Swahili sentence we need:

a. the subject prefixes
b. the tense marker
c. the verb stem, and in the case of monosyllabic verbs, the whole verb.

For example, by using the stem *soma,* "read", we can join a, b, c, together to get:

ninasoma, I read	*tunasoma,* we read
unasoma, you read	*mnasoma,* you read
anasoma, he/she reads	*wanasoma*, they read

This is the present tense. It means, in English, both "I read" and "I am reading". This becomes very clear in the verb *kwenda,* "to go":

a. *mtoto anakwenda shule kila siku*
b. *mtoto anakwenda shule sasa.*

These two sentences convey different ideas: (a) says "the child goes to school everyday", and (b) says "the child is going to school now". It is now easy to add an object: e.g. *Ninasoma kitabu kizuri,* "I am reading a nice book"; *unasoma nini?* "What are you reading?" etc.

The Perfect Tense

nimesoma, I have read	*tumesoma,* we have read
umesoma, you have read	*mmesoma,* you have read
amesoma, he has read	*wamesoma,* they have read

The Past Tense

nilisoma, I read	*tulisoma,* we read
ulisoma, you read	*mlisoma*, you read
alisoma, he, she read	*walisoma,* they read

The Future Tense

nitasoma, I shall read	*tutasoma,* we shall read
utasoma, you will read	*mtasoma,* you will read
atasoma, he/she will read	*watasoma,* they will wad

THE MONOSYLLABIC VERBS

These verbs are called monosyllabic because without the prefix *tu*, they have only one syllable each, e.g. *la, ja, fa, nywa, wa*. Taking the verb *kula,* -to eat-, we have:

Present Tense

ninakula, I eat; I am eating	*tunakula*, we eat; we are eating
unakula, you eat; you are eating	*mnakula,* you eat; you are eating
anakula , he/she eats; he is eating	*wanakula,* they eat; they are eating

Perfect Tense

nimekula, I have eaten; *tumekula*, we have eaten
umekula, you have eaten; *mmekula*, you have eaten
amekula, he/she, has eaten; *wamekula*, they have eaten

Past Tense

nimekula, I ate; *tulikula*, we ate
ulikula, you ate; *mlikula*, you ate
alikuIa, he/she ate *walikula*, they ate

Future Tense

nitakula, I shall eat; *tutakula*, we shall eat
utakula, you will eat; *mlikula*, you will eat
atakula, he/she will eat; *watakula*, they will eat

EXERCISE 16

Vocabulary

kuchuma, pick, pluck
kuona, to see
sasa, now
baadaye, afterwards
kujifunza, to learn
kwa bidii, with effort
kupiga kelele, to shout (for help etc)
kucheka, to laugh
simba, lion
tembo, elephant
twiga, giraffe
mbwa, dog
paka, cat
kueleza, to explain
kuelewa, to understand

Translate into English:

1. Wageni wamefika; mpishi anapika chakula kingi.
2. Wanawake wanapenda maua; wasichana wanachuma

maua sasa.

3. Wagonjwa wamelala; mganga amekwenda kuona simba na tembo.
4. Wezi walifungua mlango, lakini nilipiga kelele, wakakimbia.
5. Watoto wamekwenda kuona wanyama.
6. Dada amevaa nguo nzuri sana, lakini fupi.
7. Wanafunzi wanacheza sasa, watajifunza baadaye.
8. Mwalimu alieleza kila kitu na watu wote walielewa.
9. Watumishi wanachuma matunda na wanacheka sana.
10. Tulikula viazi na nyama, lakini wageni walikula ndizi.

LESSON 14

KUWA, KUWA NA, KUWAKO

THE VERB "TO BE": KUWA

This verb is irregular in the present tense. It has only one form, *ni,* for "am, is, and are". Nouns and independent personal pronouns are used with *ni* and its negative si, "am not, is not, and are not." These are:

Mimi[13] I	*sisi,* we
wewe, you (singular)	*ninyi,* you*
sisi, we	*nyinyi,* you
yeye, he, she	*wao,* they

e.g. *mimi ni mwalimu,* I am a teacher.
wewe ni mtoto, you are a child.
yeye si mwizi, he is not a thief.
sisi ni wageni Tanzania, we are strangers in Tanzania.
ninyi ni watu wema, you are kind people.
wao si walevi, they are not drunkards.

---

13 Mimi, wewe, etc... are independent personal pronouns. They are not written together with the verbs as are *ni, u, a,* etc... They may be used together with *ni, u, a,* etc... without changing the meaning of the sentence. They add emphasis: e.g. *Mimi nimeona, wewe umeona, yeye ameona,* etc... " I have seen, you has seen, she/he have seen, etc..." *Mimi* is similar to the "ego", or the italian "io".

Kuwa is regular in the perfect, past and future tenses: e.g.

Perfect Tense

nimekuwa, I have been | *tumekuwa,* we have been
utakuwa, you have been | *mmekuwa na,* you have had
amekuwa , he/she has been | *wamekuwa na,* they have had

Past Tense

nilikuwa na, I had | *tulikuwa na*, we had
ulikuwa na, you had | *mlikuwa na,* you had, etc.

Future Tense

nitakuwa, I shall be | *tutakuwa,* we shall be, etc...
utakuwa | *mtakuwa*, you will be
atakuwa | *watakuwa*

THE VERB "TO HAVE": KUWA NA

The verb *kuwa* na, like *kuwa*, is also irregular in the present tense. It is regular in all other tenses.

The Present Tense

nina, I have | *tuna,* we have
una, you have | *mna*, you have
ana, he, she has | *wana,* they have

e.g. *mtoto ana kitabu kizuri,* the child has a nice book
wana visu vikali, they have sharp knives
wagonjwa wana mganga mzuri, patients have a good doctor.

The Perfect Tense

nimekuwa na, I have had | *tumekuwa na,* we have had
umekuwa na, you have had | *mmekuwa na,* you have had
amekuwa na he/she has had | *wamekuwa na*, they have had

The Past Tense

nilikuwa, na, I had — *tulikuwa* na, we had

ulikuwa na, you had — *mlikuwa* na, you had, etc...

The Future Tense

nitakuwa na, I shall have — *tutakuwa na,* we shall have

utakuwa na, you will have etc.

TO BE IN A PLACE: KUWAKO[14]

This verb is also irregular in the present tense. In other tenses it is regular and identical with the verb *kuwa* treated above. *Kuwako* means "to be in a place". It is used to indicate that a thing or person is in a certain place, as contrasted to being in a certain state. e.g. " I am a teacher" and "I am at school " are not the same in Swahili: to be a teacher is a quality status, while to be at school is not inherent in me as a quality; I am still a teacher even when I sleep at night in my bed. This distinction of being as a status and being in a place is necessary in the present tense. In all other tenses the same form of the verb to be is used to mean to be as a status and to be in a place. The following examples will illustrate this:

Compare:	*Tatu ni mwalimu,* Tatu is a teacher.
And	*Tatu yuko shuleni,*[15] Tatu is at school.
Again	*Tatu alikuwa mtoto,* Tatu was a child.
and	*Tatu alikuwa shuleni*[15], Tatu was at school.

14 This verb is used with *yangu, yako, yake, yetu, yenu, yao*, to mean alone, e.g. *pekee yangu,* I alone, *peke yake* he/she alone, etc.

15 *shule,* "school", is derived from German "schule" , meaning "school". To express the idea of "at, in. from" school, add the suffix ni thus: *'shuleni'. Ni* is added at the end of most common nouns to express the idea of place e.g. *nyumbani,* "at home. From *nyumba,* "house."

So, too Tatu *atakuwa mama*, Tatu will be a mother.

and Tatu *atakuwa nyumbani,* Tatu will be at home.

Present Tense

niko, I am (in a place) e.g. niko hapa, I am here.
uko, you are (in a place) *uko wapi?* where are you?
yuko, he, she is (in a place) *yuko huko,* he is there.
tuko, we are (in place) *tuko,* we are here.
mko, you are (in a place) *mko ndani?* are you inside?
wako, they are (in a place) *wako huko*, they are there.

Perfect Tense

nimekuwa(ko), I have been (in a place)
umekuwa(ko), he/she has been (in a place)
amekuwa(ko), he/she has been (in a place)
tumekuwa(ko), we have been (in a place)
wamekuwa(ko), they have been (in a place)

Past Tense

nilikuwa(ko), I was (there)
ulikuwa(ko), you were (there)
alikuwa(ko), he, she was (there)
tulikuwa(ko), we were (there)
mlikuwa(ko), you were (there)
walikuwa(ko), they were (there)

Future Tense

nitakuwa(ko), I will be (there)
utakuwa(ko), you will be (there)
atakuwa(ko), he/she will be (there)
tutakuwa(ko), we will be (there)

mtakuwako(ko), you will be (there)

watakuwa(ko), they will be there

NB *ko* is often replaced by *-po-* and *mo*, thus: *mwalimu yumo*, or *yupo*, "teacher is present". In everyday language *ko* is mostly used followed by *-po* and *-mo* in order of frequency. Some authors make distinction between the uses of these terms. You may ignore such a distinction.

EXERCISE 17

Translate into Swahili:

1. Tatu is a teacher, she is at school.
2. We are children, we are at school.
3. Tatu was sick, she was at home.
4. Mother saw Tatu, she was at home.
5. They went to see Tatu, she was at home.
6. They will go to see Tatu, she will be at home.
7. Tatu has many books, she is a teacher.
8. Tatu has a good husband, he is at school.
9. Tatu has clean teeth and nice dresses.
10. Tatu eats good food, and has a strong body.

LESSON 15

WHO? WHOSE? WHICH? WHAT?

In asking questions about people, things, time or place, the following words are used:

nani? who? e.g. *nani wewe*? who are you?

wa nani? whose? mtoto *wa nani?* whose child?

watoto wa nani? whose children?

Likewise, "whose book?" *kitabu cha nani?*

whose books? *vitabu vya nani?*

It is obvious from the examples given here that "·whose" *(nani)* in Swahili takes class prefixes. It is composed of, a, "of" and *nani* "who". For more on nominal prefixes, see Lesson 20.

nini? what? e.g. anasema nini? what does he say?

wapi? where? e.g. *unakwenda wapi?* where are you going?

hapa, here; e.g. *nani yupo hapa?* who is here?

lini? when? e.g. *lini alikuja hapa*? when did he come here?

kwa nini? why? e.g. *kwa nini unachelca?* why are you laughing?

kwa sababu, because; e. g. *ninachelca kwa sababu nimefurahi,* I am laughing because I am happy.

-pi? which?	*mtoto yupi?*[16] which child?
ki/vi	*kitabu kipi?* which book?
	vitabu vipi? which books?
m/mi	mti upi? which tree?
	miti ipi? which trees?
N/N	nyumba ipi? which house?
	nyumba zipi? which houses?
J/Ma	jina lipi? which name?
	majina yapi? which names?
U	Ukuta upi ? which wall?
	kuta zipi ? which walls?
PA	pahali gani? which place?
	(Here we use another word, pahali papi is not usual. Likewise, we say, kula gani, what kind of eating?)

SOME ADVERBS OF TIME

*juzi,*day before yesterday	*mwaka jana,* last year
jana, yesterday	*mwaka uliopita,* last year
leo, today	*mwezi uliopita.* last month
kesho, tomorrow	*wiki iliyopita*, last week
kesho kutwa, day after tomorrow	*mwaka ujao,* next year
juzi na jana, day before yesterday	*mwezi ujao,* next month
juzi na jana, day before yesterday and yesterday	*wiki ijayo*. next week
juzijuzi, a few days ago	

16 The plural of mtoto *yupi*? "which child?" is not *watoto wangapi*? But *watoto gani*? "which children?" the word "*wapi*" may lead to misunderstanding, as *wapi* also means "where". So *watoto wapi*? May be mistaken for "where asre the children?"

ON THE USE OF JE

The word *je* is used to introduce a question and has no special meaning. As *no* change occurs in the structure of the sentence when asking questions in Swabili, *je,* is a useful device for calling attention to the question being asked. Compare the following two sentences, one is a question, the other is not:

a) *Mgeni amefika leo,* The guest arrived today.
b) *Je, mgeni amefika leo?* Did the guest ar rive today?

When *je* is attached to the end of the verb it means "who" "what";

e.g. *unasemaje?* how, What, do you say?
unapikaje? how do you cook?
unafanyaje? how do you do it? etc..

EXERCISE 18

Translate into Swahili:

1. The children went to school yesterday.
2. Whose wife is an excellent teacher?
3. Tatu was ill yesterday and was at home.
4. When will you go to see Tatu at home?
5. Which man is brave and kind?
6. Where were you yesterday?
7. Why is the woman cooking potatoes today?
8. You said many people will come tomorrow, how did you know?
9. How do you say (that) in Swahili?
10. A good doctor has many patients.

11. A bad doctor has few patients.
12. Who has seen an excellent cook in school?
13. How do you learn Swahili without difficulty *(bila shida)?*
14. I go to school everyday to learn Swahili. We have a very good teacher.
15. Do you have a good teacher? Do you go to school everyday? Where is the teacher now, at school or (*au*) at home?
16. I like (*penda) to* learn Swahili. It is a simple (*rahisi*) language (*lugha*).
17. I know a bit *(kidogo*) of Swahili? I can (*weza)* speak (*sema)* a little*(kidogo).*
18. Where do you learn Swahili? At home, or here?
19. I learn Swahili here, but the teacher is not (*si*) very good.
20. Which child, which book, which house?

LESSON 16

MORE ABOUT PERSONAL PRONOUNS

We have already seen two kinds of personal pronouns: a) those that stand by themselves

a. *mimi,* I — *sisi,* we
wewe, you — *ninyi,* you (pl.)
yeye, he/she — *wao,* they

b. those that are prefixed to the verbs
ni-, I — *tu-,* we
u-, you — *m-,* you (pl.)
a-, he/she — *wa-,* they

c. There is a third set of personal pronouns called "object prefixes" which denote the object governed by the verb. They are affixed immediately before the verb stem. They are:
-ni-, me, to, for me — *-tu-,* us, for, to us
-ku-, you, to, for you — *-wa-,* you, to you (pl.) them, to them,
-m, him her

Remember, when occuring before a vowel , *m* "him, etc...." becomes *mw.* e.g. *tulimwona,* "we saw her".we saw him".

The object prefix *m* for "you" plural is no longer used; *wa* has replaced it. You can tell from the context whether *wa* refers to " you", or to "them." If, for example, you are talking to many people and you say to them: *ninawaona*, you certainly mean" I see you " (pl.).

Sometimes *ku* and *ni* are used to denote the object prefix for "you", plural , thus: *ninakuoneni,* "I see you" or also *ninawaoneni,* "I see you". When *ni* suffixes the verb, the final *a* is changed into *e*, as is clear from the examples given above.

EXERCISE 19

Insert the right object prefix from the brackets:

4. Nili———ona jana (ni, ku).
5. Juzi nilikuwa hapa, nani ali ——— ona (m, ni)?
6. Mwalimu amekuja shuleni, je, ume ———ona (ku, ni, mw)?
7. Wageni walikuwa hapa, tuli———ona (ku, ni, wa, mw)?
8. Wagonjwa watakuja, mganga ata ——— ona (ni, m, wa).
9. Je, baba ali——— ambia nini mama (ni , ku, mw)?
10. Je, ali ——— ambia nini sisi (ku, m, tu wa)?
11. Je, dada atakuja lini? Ninataka ku———ona (tu, wa, mw).
12. Ninataka ku———ambia kitu wewe (m, ni , ku, wa).
13. Ninajua kila kitu, unataka ku———ambia nini (ku, m, ni)?

Vocabulary

kuuliza, to ask	*swali, ma-* question
kueleza, to explain	*jibu, ma-* answer
kutazama, to look at	*maelezo*, explanation
kupenda, to love, like	*majaribio,* trial
kuchukia, to hate	*chuki,* hatred
kujibu, to answer	*mapendo*, love, liking
kujaribu, to try	*tendo, ma-* deed, action
kuharibu, to destroy	*uchungu*, bitterness

EXERCISE 20

ON ASKING QUESTIONS

Translate into English:

Tatu alituuliza swali moja gumu sana, tukajaribu kumjibu. Sisi pia tulimwuliza swali moja gumu, na yeye akajaribu kutujibu. Tatu anapenda sana kuuliza watu maswali magumu. Kila siku anawauliza maswali mengi. Watu wengi wanapenda kuuliza wenzao maswali (wenzi wao: *companions).* Kuuliza ni njia nzuri ya kujifunza vitu vingi. Kuuliza si ujinga.

LESSON 17

THE SWAHILI NEGATIVE FORMS

Swahili uses a different set of subject prefixes to express negations. The idea of negation is contained in these subject prefixes. They are:

a. in the M-W A class:

si, I, not	hatu, we ..... not
hu, you... not	ham, you ... not
ha, he, she... not	hawa, they .....not

b. in other classes:

M/MI, hau/hai,	e.g. mti *hau*... miti hai...anguki
KI/VI, haki/havi,	kiti *haki*... viti havi... fai
N/N, hai/hazi,	nyumba *hai*... vyumba hazi...toshi
O/MA, hali/haya,	jina *hali*... majina haya...maana
U, hau/hazi,	uso *hau* ... nyuso hazi..... sura
PA, hapa,	pahali *hapa* ....fai
KU, haku,	kusoma *haku*...

The following rules apply to the formation of negatives in Swahili :

i. All verbs drop *ku* of the infinitives in all the tenses, only the monosyllabic verbs retain the *ku* in the future tense.

ii. Verbs ending in *a* or *e* change these final vowels into *i* in the present tense only.

iii. *na* which shows the present tense in the affirmative statements is not replaced at all, but *me* is replaced by *ja, li by ku,* and *ta* remains unchanged.

Swahili tenses in the affirmative and in the negative:

Affirmative	**Negative**
kusoma, to read	*kutokusoma*, not to read
(Affirm)	**(Neg.)**

The Present Tense

sisomi, I do not read	*ninasoma,* I read
unasoma, you read	*husomi,* you do noto read
anasoma, he/ she reads	*hasomi*, he/she does not read

The Perfect Tense

nimesoma, I have read	*sijasoma,* I have not read
umesoma, you have read	*hujasoma,* you have not read
amesoma, he/she has read	*hajasoma,* he/she has not read

The Past Tense

nilisoma, I read	*sikusoma*, I did not read
ulisoma, you read	*hukusoma,* you did not read
alisoma, he read	*hakusoma,* he/she did not read
tulisoma, we read	*hatukusoma*, we did not read
mlisoma, you read	*hamkusoma*, you did not read
walisoma, they read	*hawakusoma*, they did not read

The Future Tense

nitasoma, I shall read	*sitasoma*, I shall not read
utasoma, you will read	*hutasoma*, you will not read
atasoma, he will read	*hatasoma,* she/he will not read
tutasoma, we shall read	*hatutasoma*, we will not read
mtasoma, you will read	*hamtasoma,* you will not read
watasoma. they will read	*hawatasoma*,they will not read

A few examples from the monosyllabic verbs:

The Present Tense

ninakula, I eat — *sili*, I do not eat
unakula, you eat — *huli*, you do not eat

The Perfect Tense

nimekula, I have eaten — *sijala.* I have not eaten
umekula, you have eaten — *hujala*, you have not eaten, etc...

The Past Tense

nilikula, I ate — *sikula*, I did not eat
ulikula, you ate — *hukula*, you did not eat

The Future Tense

nitakula, I shall eat — *Sitakula*, I did not eat
utakula, you will eat — *hutakula*, you will not eat

Similarly *kuja*, "to come" has:

ninakuja, I am coming — *siji*, I am not coming
unakuja, you are coming — *huji*, you are not coming

The Perfect Tense

nimekuja, I have come — *sijaja*, I have not come

The Past Tense

nilikuja, I came — *sikuja*, I did not come

The Future Tense

Nitakuja, I shall come — *sitakuja*,I shall not come etc.

EXERCISE 21

Change the following affirmative sentences/clauses into the negative and the negative into the affirmative, after this model:

Je, mwalimu amekuja? (affirmative)

Je, mwalimu hajaja? (negative)

1. Nani anakula ndizi za mtoto?
2. Wageni wanapenda samaki, lakini hawataki ndizi.
3. Baba amekuja na amelala.
4. Mwalimu alisema wewe ni mtoto mjanja,
5. Mgonjwa hali samaki, anakula viazi na mkate.
6. Nani alikuja hapa jana?
7. Je, umeona simba? Nani hajaona simba?
8. Mganga atakuja kesho.

The negative forms of " *kuwa...*" "*kuwa na..*" and "*kuwako*"

The negative forms of the verbs *kuwa*, "to be", *kuwa na*, "to have", and *kuwako*, "to be in a place", differ only in the present tense. Thus:

Affirmative	Negative
Kuwa	
ni, am, is, are	*si*, am not, is not, are not
Kuwa na	
nina, I have	*sina*, I have not
una, you have	*huna*, you have not
ana, he/she has	*hana*, she has not
wana, they have	*hawana*, they have not

Kuwako

niko, I am (in a place)	*siko*, I am not (in a place)
uko, you are...	*huko*, you are not
yuko, he/she is...	*hayuko*, he/she is not
wako, they are...	*hawako*, they are not
tuko, we are...	*hatuko*, we are not
niko, you are....	*Huko*, I, you are not
tuko, we are...	*hatuko*, we are not
mko, you are	*hamko*, you are not

Perfect Tense

sijawa: I have not been e.g. *sijawa mjinga hivyo*: "I have not become such a fool"

kuwako does not appear in this tense;

kuwa na: sijawa na, I have not had, e.g. *sijawa na mali nyingi sana*, "I have not yet (acquired) much wealth".

The Past Tense

kuwa: sikuwa, I was not, etc...

kuwako, sikuwa(ko), I was not i n a place, e tc....

kuwa na: sikuwa na, I did not have, or I had not, etc....

Future Tense

kuwa: sitakuwa, I shall not be, etc....

kuwako, sitakuwa, I shall not be in a place....

kuwa na: sitakuwa na, I shall not have, etc....

LESSON 18

ORDERS AND WISHES

In Swahili orders are given by using the verb stem or in the case of monosyllabic verbs, the whole verb, e.g.

soma, read

andika, write

lala, sleep, lie down

kula, eat (monosyllabic verb)

kunywa, drink (monosyllabic)

Kuja is irregular, its imperative is *njoo*, "come". Commands in the plural are given by suffixing *ni* to the singular form and changing the final *a* into *e* as follows:

Singular	**Plural**
soma, read	*Someni,* read (you)
andika, write	*andikeni*, write (you)
kula, eat	*kuleni* (eat) you
njoo, come	*njooni,* come you

Wishes similar to the English, "let me,· "let us" , are expressed by using the verb stem, changing the *final a* into *e,* and adding the personal pronominal prefixies: *ni, u, a tu, m-, wa*

Thus, taking the verb *kuenda*, "to go", we have:

niende, I may go, let me go. *Je, niende*? May I go?

uende, you may go, go

aende, let him, her go

twende, let us go, we may go
mwende, you may go, go
waende, let them go, they may go

Monosyllabic verbs form no exception here, so we have:

nije, let me come, I may come...
uje, you may come
aje, he/she may (should) come
tuje, we may come, we should come
mje, you may come, should come
waje, let them come, they may come

Likewise, *nile,* "let me eat"; *ule,* "you may eat" , etc. This form is called subjunctive. It is used whenever intention is expressed. The first verb is said to be in the indicative and the second in the subjunctive mood. e.g.

Alinipa kitabu nisome, he gave me a book to read.
Anakula chakula bora apate nguvu, he eats good (excellent) food to get strength.
Walituita twende kula, they called us to go and eat

The subjunctive is used after certain verbs, like:

kuambia, to tell
kusema, to say
kuita, to call

e.g. *Nilimwambia aje,* I told him to come.
Je, alisema twende leo? Did he say we should go today?
Ita wageni waje kula, Call the guests to come and eat

With words like, *lazima*, it is necessary

inafaa, it is better, useful

haifai, it is not good, useless

ni vizuri, it is good

si vizuri, it is not good

e.g. *Lazima uende nyumbani*, You must go home.

lnafaa uende nyumbani, It is better you go home.

Ni vizuri uende, It is good that you go home.

With imperatives:

e.g. *njoo nikuambie*, come I will tell you something.

ngoja aje, wait (until) he comes.

sema nifanye nini? say what I should do.

njoo tunywe pombe, come, let us drink beer.

karibu tule, welcome, let us eat

With verbs implying prohibition or refusal, such as:

kukataza, to forbid

kukataa, to refuse

kuzuia, to prevent

These verbs take the negative subjunctive, which is as fol lows:

nisiende, that I may not go

usiende, that you may not go, don't go

asiende, that he/she may not go

tusiende, that we may not go, let us not go

msiende, that you may not go, don't go

wasiende, that they may not go, let them not go

e.g. *Baba alitukataza tusiende shambani*, Father forbade us going into the field.

The negative subjunctive is formed by inserting *si* between the subject prefix and the verb stem, as shown above. So, the affirmative and negative subjenctives differ because of this *si*. but the form is the same in both.

Compare:

niende, I may go, let me go
nisiende , let me not go
tuende, let us go
tusiende, let us not go

The negative subjunctive is used to express orders or commands in the second person. Thus:

usiende, don't go
msiende, don't go (pl.)
usije kesho, do not come tomorrow
msije kesho, do not come tomorrow
usile matunda mabichi. don' t eat unripe fruit
msile matunda mabichi, don ' t eat unripe fruit
usifanye hivi, do not do this
msifanye hivi, do not do this
usiwe na shaka. do not have doubts
msiwe na shaka, do not have doubts
usijali, do not mind
msijali, do not mind
usinisumbue, do not bother me
msinisumbue, do not bother me

When orders and wishes contain an object prefix the final *a* of the verbs is changed into *e.*

e.g. *niambie,* "tell me"; *mwambie,* "tell him ".

Likewise: *usinitazame hivyo*, **"do not look at me like that." Some verbs take on an additional vowel before the final** *a* **when they include indirect objetts. Here are a few examples:**

kuleta, to bring	*kuletea*, to bring to, for
kuandika, to write	*kuwaandikia,* to write to, for
kusoma, to read	*kusomea*, to read to, for
kutaka, to want	*kutakia*, to wish someone
kufanya, to do	*kufanyia*, to do to, for
kukataa, to refuse	*kukatalia,* to refuse to
kufikiri, to think	*kufikiria,* to think of, for
kusema, to say	*kusemea,* to speak for

We may conclude from the above examples that:

a. Whenever the vowel immediately preceding the final syllable is *e* or *o*, then *e* is inserted. Thus: *kuleta*, becomes *kuletea*, and *kusoma* becomes kusomea;
b. If the vowel preceding the last syllable is *i* then *i* is inserted. e.g. *kuandika* becomes *kuandikia;*
c. If the preceding vowel is *a, i* is again inserted before the last vowel, e.g. *kutaka* becomes *kutakia.*

Observe the different meanings conveyed by these verbs when they take on additional vowels. e.g. *kutaka* to want: *anataka chai* he wants tea; *kutaka* to wish somebody(well, ill). *Nakutakia heri,* "I wish you all good things ! "Ninakutaka, " I want you".

d. Verbs ending in *ua*, insert *li* before the final *a*. *kufungua* "to open", becomes *kufungulia,* "to open for someone".

amefungua mlango, "he has opened the door"; but *amenifungulia mlango*,
"he has opened the door for, to me".

e. Verbs ending in - *i* add *a* at the end, e.g. *kufikiri*, "to think", becomes *kufikiria*,
"to think of, about, consider". Examples:
Baba alifikiri sana. Father thought hard
Baba alikujikiria sana. Father thought of you very much
Alirudi jana jioni. He came back yesterday evening
Alirudia somo lake. He repeated his lesson

f. Verbs ending *in -w*, insert *li* before the final *a*, e.g. *kukimbia*, "to run", becomes *kukimbilia*, "to run after".

Observation: The above rules serve for both affirmative and negative orders and wishes. Examples:

Niletee chai, Bring me tea
Usiniletee chai, Don't bring me tea
Mpe mtoto maziwa, Give the child milk
Usimpe mtoto maziwa, Do not give the child milk
Mwambie aje, Tell him to come
Usimwambie aje, Don't tell him to come
Uwe hapa kesho asubuhi, Be here tomorrow morning
Usiwe hapa kesho asubuhi, Don't be here tomorrow moming

EXERCISE 22

Answer the following questions in the negative:

e.g. *Je, mwalimu wetu alikuja jana shuleni?*

Answer: *Hapana, mwalimu wetu hakuja shuleni jana.*

1. Je, mwalimu amekuja?
2. Je, unakula samaki na viazi?
3. Je, mlevi anakunywa pombe kila siku?
4. Je, mlikuwa nyumbani jana?
5. Je, ulinifikiria au hapana?

EXERCISE 23

Translate into Swahili:

1. A good name, good names.
2. Where are you going? I am going home.
3. Do not go home now, let us go to play.
4. I must go home now; mother has forbidden me to play.
5. Eat one banana, it is very sweet.
6. I do not eat bananas at school.
7. Whose books are you reading now? Teacher's books?
8. I am reading sister's books, they are very nice and easy.
9. What are you laughing at? Are you laughing at me?
10. How do you know I am laughing at you? I am not laughing.
11. You should not laugh at people.
12. Do not come to see me tomorrow, I won't be at home. Come the day after tomorrow, I will be at home.
13. Goodbye, I must now go home safely (salama).
14. Goodbye, I'll see you tomorrow. (lit. We shall see each other tomorrow).

EXERCISE 24

Complete these sentences and then change them into the negative forms.

1. Wageni wa... (kufika) jana.
2. Watoto wa... (kufanya) nini sasa?
3. Wagonjwa wa... (kuenda) hospitali kesho.
4. Nani ali... (kusema) maneno mabaya jana?
5. Je, ulimwona mwalimu? Ndiyo ni...
6. Je, mama (kuwako) wapi sasa? Mama... (kuwako) jikoni sasa.
7. Je, u... (kula) viazi sasa? Ndiyo ni... (kula viazi sasa).
8. Njoo tu... (kula) ; niletee maji (kunywa).
9. Je, wanafunzi wame... (kufika)? Ndiyo wanafunzi wa...
10. Je, mna... (kutaka) nini hapa? Tu... (kutaka) kazi.

LESSON 19

DEMONSTRATIVES: THIS AND THAT

This, that and their plurals these and those are called demonstratives, from the Latin *demonstrare*, to show. In Swahili, demonstratives are of three kinds: Those that point to somebody, or something near; those that indicate persons or things far away; and those that show people, or things that are nearer to the person spoken to than they are to the speaker. Let us begin with demonstratives that refer to people.

Singular	Plural
mtu huyu, this man (person)	*watu hawa*, these men (people)
mtu yule, that man	*watu wale*, these men
mtu huyo, that man (near your)	*watu hao*, those men there (near you)

Huyo and *hao* are used also to refer to persons about whom we have already spoken. They may also be used to show contempt, e.g. *mtu huyu ni mjinga*, "such a man is a fool". When pursuing a thief, people cry *mwizi huyo!* "there runs the thief! watch out".

Suppose I see you walking with a child and I want to know whose child it is, what form should I use? Of course, *huyo* I should say: *Mtoto huyo ni wa nani*? "Whose child is that (near you)? " Suppose again, we are walking together and we see a child some distance away from us, what form should I use in pointing to the child? No doubt, yule: *Mtoto yule ni wa nani?* "Whose child is that there?" And if the child is near to both of us, I should say: *Mtoto huyu.*

Below is a list of Swahili demonstratives for different noun classes: (The symbol ø means *naught* or nil)

NOUN CLASS

M/MI	*mti huu,* this tree,	*mti ule,* that tree
	miti hii, these trees,	*miti ile,* those trees
KI/VI	*kitabu hiki* this book	*kitablu kile,* that book
	vitabu hivi, these books	*vitabu vile,* those books
øMA	*jina hili,* this name	*jina lile,* that name
	majina haya, these names	*majina yale,* those names
N/N	*nyumba hii,* this house	*Nyumba ile, that house*
	nyumba hizi, these houses	*nyumba zile,* those houses
U	*ukuta huu this wall*	*ukuta ule,* that wall
	kuta hizi,	*kuta hizi,* those walls,
PA	*pahali hapo,* this place	*pahali pale,* that place
KU	*kula huku,* this eating	*kula kule* that eating

For the third demonstrative *(huyo),* we have;

M/MI	*mti huo, that tree (near you), or such a tree...*
	miti hiyo, these trees (near you), or such trees...
KI/VI	*kitabu hicho that book (near you), or such a book...*
	vitabu hivi, those books (near you) or such books...
MA	*jina hilo, such a name*
	majina hayo such names
N/N	*nyumba hiyo, that house (near you), such a house*
	nyumba hizo, those houses, such houses
U	*ukuta huo, that wall (near you), such a wall*
	kuta hizo, those walls,
PA	*pahali hapo , that place (near you)*
KU	*kula huko, this eating , or such eating*

LESSON 20

POSSESSIVE PRONOUNS

In Swahili the possessive pronouns are treated like adjectives. They take nominal prefixes, as shown below:

-angu, my, mine	*-etu,* our, ours
-ako, your, yours	*-enu,* your, yours
-ake, his, her, hers	*-ao* their, theirs

The following are the class prefixes:

NOUN CLASS

M/WA, W	*mtoto wangu,* my child
	watoto wangu, my children
M/MI, W/Y	*mkono wake*, her hand
N/N, Y/Z	*mikono yake*, her hands
	kitabu chako, your book
V/N, W/Z	*vitabu vyako*, your books
PA , P	*nyumba yetu*, our house
KU, KW	*nyumba zetu*, our house
	Jina langu, my name
ØMA, L/Y	*majina yangu*, my names
U	*ufunguo wake*, their keys
	funguo zao, their keys
PA, P	*Pahali pake*, your place
KU, KW	*Kusoma kwake*, his reading

The same prefixes are used to express "of" – *a*: For the *m/wa* class, "of" is denoted by *wa* for both singular and plural.

e.g. *mtoto wa mwalimu*, the teacher's child
watoto wa mwalimu,the teacher's children
for the *ki/vi* class, you have:
kitabu cha mwalimu, the teacher's book.
vitabu vya mwalimu. the teacher's books

Once you know that "of" is *-a* in *Swahili*, you can use it with the prefixes given above without any difficulty.

EXERCISE 25

Supply the right prefixes:

1. Je, nani ameona vitabu -a mwalimu leo?
2. Wageni wameleta mizigo -ao.
3. Walikuwa na mizigo -ingi sana na -zito.
4. Nyumba -etu ni kubwa na nzuri, ina milango -wili.
5. Wape funguo -ao, funguo -ako ziko wapi?
6. Majina -a watoto hawa ni rnagumu lakini mazuri.
7. Miguu -ake ni mizuri kuliko miguu -a dada yake.
8. Kusoma -ake si kuzuri lakini kuandika -ake ni kuzuri.
9. Mkono -a mtoto mdogo ni -dogo,
   na kichwa -ake ni -dogo pia.
10. Je, umemwona mtoto -angu? Alikuwa na (with) watoto -ako.

EXERCISE 26

Translate into Swahili:

1. His children are not going to school today.
2. Our teacher does not eat at school, he eats at home.
3. Where do you go to eat? I do not eat here.
4. Their cook is not coming today.
5. Tell him to come the day after tomorrow.
6. Where are our books? Where are our clothes?
7. I heard people shout: Thief! Thief! There goes the thief!
8. Who is that man? That man is our guest.
9. Whose child is this? This child is hers.
10. Who are those people? Those people are our guests.
11. Bring me that child (near you), I want to see him.
12. May I go now? I have no work. Go and do not come again to bother me.

LESSON 21

THE CONDITIONAL TENSES

Swahili has four distinct tenses which express condition. They are formed with:

a. *-ki-* "if" to denote a simple condition. The word *kama* is sometimes used to introduce the conditional tense: it may, however, be omitted, as *-ki-* by itself also expresses condition.

e.g. *Kama ukitaka mali fanya kazi, or ukitaka mali* "If you want wealth, work."

Note the position of *ki* it is placed immediately after the subject prefix. This is its permanent position. Note again that all verbs without exception drop the *ku.* Even the monosyllabic verbs are not exempted, e.g. *Ukila chakula bora utakuwa na nguvu,* "If you eat good food you will be strong" *Ukija kesho utanikuta hapa,* "If you come tomorrow you will find me here."

b. *ki,* is also used to connect two actions, the second verb taking the *ki;* e.g.

Tulimsikia akiimba, We heard her/him singing.

Nilimkuta akisoma, I found him reading.

c. *japo, ijapokuwa,* "even if": *Japo mtoto akilia, usimpe maziwa,* "Even if the child cries do not give him milk".

d) *nge, ngali*: These denote a condition not likely to be fulfilled. e.g. *Kama ningekuwa na fedha ningenunua gari,*

"If I had money I would buy a car". In spoken language *nge* and *ngali* are interchangeable.

CONDITIONAL NEGATIVES

Conditional negative tenses are expressed by *-sipo-*, "if not" e.g. *Usipotaka kujenga ukuta ziba ufa,* "If you do not want to build a wall stop up the crack". *Asipokuja, basi nenda nyumbani,* "If he does not come then go home".

The *-nge-* is replaced by *-singe-* and –ngali by *-singali-* e.g. *Kama wangekuja tusingewaona* "Had they not come we would not have seen them."

Swahili has another way of expressing conditional tenses by using the negative subject prefixes followed by *nge* or *ngali.*

e.g. *singesoma (singalisoma),* had I not read....
hungesoma (hangalisoma), had he not read....
hangesoma (Hangalisoma), had he not read....

Likewise:

Miti isingeanguka, nyunba yetu haingeanguka.
Our house would not fall if the trees did not fall.
Kisu hakingevunjika, The knife would not break.
Visu havingevunjika, The knives would not break.

The first form is more frequent and probably simpler than this one. Choose the form you prefer and learn it well.

EXERCISE 27

Translate into English:

1. Kama ungefika jana ungemkuta mgeni wetu hapa.
2. Kama akitoa fedha mpe kitabu hiki.
3. Kama asipotoa fedha usimpe kitabu hiki.
4. Kama watu wengi wakitaka kitu basi wape.
5. Tulikwenda shuleni, tulimkuta mwalimu akisoma kitabu kile.
6. Kama huli samaki watakupikia ndizi kwa nyama.
7. Ngoja nikupe habari za mlevi yule.
8. Asingeniambia ningoje, nisingengoja (*or* singengoja).

LESSON 22

THE PASSIVE VOICE

Consider the following sentences:

a. Tatu loves her children.

b. Tatu is loved by her children.

In both sentences Tatu is the subject but she is not the doer in the second sentence. She is said to be passive. This is the passive voice. The first sentence is in the active voice. Tatu is the doer, i.e. she loves... In Swahili, the passive voice is rendered by *wa* added at the end of the verb following the rules given below:

1. Verbs ending in *-a, -ea* and *-ia*, insert *w* before the final vowel *a*. e.g. *kupenda* "to love"; *kupendwa* "to be loved". Now you know how to translate sentence (b) above. Remember the English verb is is not translated in the Swahili verb. Thus *Tatu anapendwa na watoto wake* is the rendering of (b). If you analyse the Swahili rendering you will see that the conjunction *na* stands for the English "by" although it also means "and".

2. Verbs ending in *-aa, ua,* insert *liw* before the final *a*. e.g. *kukataa*, "to refuse";*-amekataa,* "he has refused", *kukataliwa,* "to be refused"; *amekataliwa,* " he has been refused".

3. Verbs ending in *-au* add *liwa* at the end: e.g. *kusahau*, to forget; *kusahauliwa,* "to be forgotten".

4. Verbs ending in *e* and i add *wa* at the end: e. g. *kusamehe*, "to forgive" ; *kusamehewa*, "to be forgiven".

5. Verbs ending in *oa*insert kw before the last *a.* e.g. *kuoa*, to marry (man) ; *kuolewa*, to be married (woman).

6. Verbs ending in *u* drop the *u* and add *wa:* e.g. *kujibu*, "to answer"; *kujibiwa*, "to be answered."

The doer in the passive voice is called the agent. In the sentence *Tatu anapendwa na watoto wake*, Tatu's children are the agents, they do the act of loving while their mother receives the act of loving. Consider this sentence also: *Dada anapendwa na kila mtu* "(My) sister is loved by every one".

To express the agent Swahili uses the word *na* as already pointed out. If however the action is accomplished by means of an instrument, Swahili uses the word *kwa* to express the idea of instrumentality.

e.g. *Aliandika barua kwa wino*, He wrote a letter with (in) ink.
Alipigwa kwa fimbo, He was hit with a stick.
Walipigwa mawe, They were stoned.

In the last example the word *kwa* has been omitted, but it is understood. The sentence should more correcdy read: *walipigwa kwa mawe.*

EXERCISE 28

Change the following sentences into the passive voice:

Active	Passive
Mtoto amejibu swali.	*Swali limejibiwa na mtoto.*
The child has answered the question.	The question has been answered by the child.

1. Tuliwapokea wageni wengi jana.
2. Watoto wanampenda sana mwalimu wao.
3. Bahati ameandika barua nzuri kwa wino.
4. Watu wengi wamesahau jambo hili sasa.
5. Waziri amewafikiria wafanyakazi wote.
6. Nani amefungua mlango wa chumba changu?
7. Baba alikata mti ule mrefu kwa shoka.
8. Wezi walivunja nyumba ile nzuri ya mwalimu wetu usiku. (Wezi walivunja usiku nyumba ila nzuri ya mwalimu wetu).
9. Mbwa alipasua nguo ya Bahati kwa makucha yake makali.
10. Mama alikataza watoto wasicheze chumbani.

The passive voice in the negative offers no special difficulty. It follows the same rules as in the affirmative. Thus:

Bahati anapendwa, Bahati is loved

*Bahati hapendwi (*passive), Bahati is not loved

Bahati alipendwa, Bahati was loved

Bahati hakupendwa, Bahati was not loved

Bahati atapendwa, Bahati will be loved

Bahati hatapendwa, Bahati will not be loved

Useful Phrases

Mtoto alizaliwa mwaka 1970.	The child was born in 1970.
Tatu aliolewa na.....	Tatu was married to...
Tatu alisifiwa kwa kazi yake nzuri,	Tatu was praised for her good work.
Sitaki nguo hizo, zimevaliwa na mtu fulani,	I do not like those clothes, they have been worn by a certain person.
Mwizi amekamatwa na polisi,	The thief has been arrested by the police.
Gari limeharibika,	The car is out of order
Wezi walipigwa mawe na...	The thieves were stoned by....
Jambo hili haliwezekani,	This matter is impossible.
Sukari haipatikani hapa,	The sugar is not available here.

LESSON 23

THE EKA AND IKA TENSES

The *eka* and *ika* tenses denote a state; something has been done to the subject but no agent or doer is expressed. Observe the following sentences and note the difference between the stative and the passive forms:

Kisu kimevunjwa na mpishi.	The knife has been broken by a cook (passive).
Kisu kimevunjika,	The knive has broken (stative)
Nguo imeraruliwa na mbwa,	Her dress was torn by a dog (passive).
Nguo yake imeraruka,	Her dress is torn(stative).

Children especially like this form because it does not implicate them. e.g. A child says: *mama, kikombe kimevunjika* "mother, the cup is broken"; not *mama. nimevunja kikombe,* "mother, I have broken the cup"

SWAHILI AUXILIARY VERBS

In Swahili two verbs are used as auxiliary verbs, namely, *kuwa*[16], "to be- and k*uisha* "to be completed ". This last verb is used as an auxiliary verb meaning "already."

e.g.	*Alikuwa akisoma tulipofika shuleni,*	He was reading when we arrived at school.
	Sasa baba atakuwa amefika.	By now father will have arrived.

KUISHA[17]

Wageni wamekwisha fika,	The guests have already arrived.
Je, umekwisha ona simba?	Have you seen a lion?
Nimekwisha kukwambia,	I have already told you.

It should not be concluded from the examples given above that all verbs ending in *ka* are stative. A few examples will show you that this is not the case. Consider:

kupika, to cook,	*kupika ndizi,* to cook bananas
kuzika, to bury	*kuzika maiti.* to bury a dead man
kuandika, to write	*kuandika barua*, to write a letter
kufunika, to cover	*kufunika kitu,* to cover up something
kutandika, to set in order	*kutandika kitanda,* to make a bed
kuweka, to put,	*weka sahani mezani*, put the plates on the table
kushika, to hold.	*wameshika mwizi*, they have

16 *Kuwa* is not used as anxiliary in present tense.
17 After *kuisha* you may use the verb with *ku* (all verbs)

	caught the thief
kuezeka, to thatch.	*kuezeka nyumba,* to thatch a house
kuvika, to dress.	*vika mtoto nguo*, dress the child
kucheka, to laugh.	*usimcheke maskini*, do not laugh at a poor man
kupaka ,to smear.	*kupaka nyumba rangi*, to paint a house
Kuteka, to draw (water)	*kuteka maji*, to draw water
kupeleka, to send.	*peleka barua hii posta*, send this letter to the post office.
Kulimbika, to save up.	*inafaa kulimbika mali,* it is good to save up some wealth

LESSON 24

THE IMPERSONAL AND THE RECIPROCAL FORMS OF VERBS

kuna, mna, pana, **"there is, there are"**

kuna shows an indefinite position. *mna* denotes a place inside something. while *pana* refers to a definite place.

e.g. *Kuna watu shuleni*, there are people in the school.
Mna watu chumbani, there are people in the room.
Pana mtu dirishani, there is someone at the window.

The negative is formed by prefixing *ha*, thus: *hakuna, hamna, hapana,* "there is not, there are not". In the affirmative not the common form is *kuna,* and in the negative, *hamna,* while *hapana* now means " no". *Siyo* "no", is slowly falling out of use and being replaced by *hapana.* Note that *mna* is not used in exactly the same way as the English " in". *Mna* denotes definite insideness, as in a room, a hole, a bag, etc.... A Swahili speaker would not use *mna* to refer to being "in a country, in a river, etc..."

In practice, however, the Swahili do not pay attention to such distinctions as have been pointed out above. *Kuna* seems to cover every case in the affirmative, and *hamna* in the negative, as already observed.

Inafaa " it is useful, good" (followed by subjunctive)

e. g. *Inafaa twende sasa,* it is better we go now.

Haifai twende sasa (Negative), it is not good that we go now.
lnawezekana, it is possible.
Haiwezekani, it is not possible.
lnatosha, it is enough.
Haitoshi, (Negative), it is not enough.
Si kitu, it is nothing, it does not matter.
Haidhuru, it does not matter, it is nothing.

Pasa, bidii, lazima

Pasa, bidii, and *lazima* express the idea of necessity, compulsion, duty, etc.

e.g. *yanipasa/yanibidi kwenda*, I must go.
*Unapaswa/linakubidi kwend*a, you must go.
Inampasa/inambidi kwenda, he/she must go, etc.
ni lazima watoto waende shule, it is necessary that children go to school.

EXERCISE 29

Translate into Swahili:

1. You had better learn Swabili.
2. Children must go to school now.
3. What are you doing? I am learning Swahili
4. It is enough, let us go to see friends.
5. I must Iearn Swahili everyday, I want to know it. It is possible to know it in two months.
6. Who is your teacher? Do you bave good books?
7. There are no good books in the shops.

8. Our teacher is writing a book for you.
9. I do not know your teacher, what is his name?
10. Do you want to see him? Come tomorrow, you will see him. He also wants to see you.
11. It does not matter; it is not necessary to see him.
12. It is possible to learn Swahili without a teacher.

EXERCISE 30

Rewrite the following sentences using the correct forms of the words in brackets:

1. Sukari hai... (kupatikana) hapa siku hizi.
2. Wezi wame... (kukamata) na polisi.
3. Kazi hii hai... (kuwezekana) leo.
4. Macho yake haya... (kuona) vizuri sasa.
5. Je, mtoto wako ali... (kuzaa) lini?
6. Je, unataka sisi tu... (kuenda) wapi kesho?
7. Haifai watoto... (kucheza) shuleni, lazima (kujifunza).
8. Je, alisema watumishi... (kufanya) nini?
9. Je, wageni ha... (kula) sasa?
10. Je, uki... (kuona) simba utafanya nini?
11. Mwambie mpishi... (kuja) hapa, nataka a... (kuonyesha mimi) chakula cha leo.
12. Mama alisema ninyi... (kula) ndizi kila siku.
13. Mzee alisema ni (kusoma) barua hii, sijui kusoma.
14. Mgonjwa anasema ha... (kuja) kula leo, mpelekee chakula.

Soma Useful Expressions

Kuna nini?	What is the matter?
Hamna kitu,	There is nothing.
Hapakuwa na mtu,	There was nobody.
Pana mtu mbele,	There is somebody in front.
Nani yuko nyuma?	Who is behind?
Hamna taabu.	No problem, don't mind!
Nipe kitabu nisome,	Give a book to read.
Nipe maji ninywe,	Give me some water to drink.
Mpe mtoto ndizi ale,	Give the child bananas to eat.

THE RECIPROCAL FORMS OF THE VERBS

Mutual actions are expressed in Swabili by adding *na* to the end of the verb. e.g. *kupenda*, "to love, like"; *kupendana.* to like each other-. If the verb ends in *e* add *ana,' kusamehe,* "to forgive"; kusameheana "to forgive each other. "

If the verb ends in *i* and *ana* e.g. *kurudi,* "to return"; *kurudiana* "to return to one another" (i.e. to be reconciled).

If a verb ends in *u* change the *u* into i and add *ana,* e.g.

kujibu, "to answer" *kujibizana.* "to answer to each other."

Kusifu, "to praise"; *kusifiana.* "to praise one another"

Here are some of the commonest verbs and their reciprocals:

ona, see	*onana,* meet, see each other
kosa, do wrong, miss	*kosana*, disagree, quarrel
jua	*kujuana*, know each other
pata, get	*patana,* agree, be friendly
fuana, follow	*fuatana,* follow one another
amkia, greet	*amkiana*, greet each other
ambia, tell	*ambiana*, tell one another
gomba, scold	*gombana*, scold each other

piga, hit — *pigana*, fight each other
epa, avoid — *epana*, avoid each other
vuta, pull — *vutana*, pull one another

When the reciprocal *na* is added to the *-em* and *-ilea* forms, it does not change the meaning of that verb form, but forms a stative verb:

kuoneka (not used) — *kuonekana*, to be seen, visible
kujulika (not used), — *kujulikana*, to be known
kupatika (not used) — *kupatikana*, to be available
kuwezeka (not used) — *kuwezekana*, to be possible

EXERCISE 31

Translate into Swahili:

1. The thief has been seen in town.
2. It is not possible to go now, let us wait a little.
3. He is well known and loved by many people.
4. The women whom you saw yesterday are not on good terms.
5. I do not know why they quarrelled.
6. It is good to greet each other when you meet.
7. It is bad to fight or to scold one another.
8. Tatu had separated from her husband, but they have now rejoined.
9. These two children like each other very much, they follow each other everywhere.
10. Friends often write each other long letters.
11. Cover your food because flies like your food, too.
12. Who makes your bed every morning?
13. Dress the child quickly, we must go now.
14. Why did they laugh at the stranger?
15. What are you cooking today? I do not eat fish.

LESSON 25

THE RELATIVES

We have already discussed the interrogatives: nani? "who?" nini? ·what?" -a nani" whose? -ipi? "which?" etc.

Let us look at the relatives. Consider these sentences:

a. The man you saw yesterday is my father.

b. The book which you gave me is very, very nice.

In the first sentence we left out one word, namely, "whom". "The man whom you saw..." The words "whom" in the first sentence and which in the second are called relative pronouns.

Swahili has two ways of expressing relative pronouns. It either attaches the relative particle to the verb or it uses the word *amba* to which it attaches the relative particles. Here are some examples of each:

a. With the M/W A class, *ye (*abbreviation of *yeye)* is used in the singular and o (abbreviation of *wao*) is used in the plural.

e.g. *Mtu uliyemwona jana ni baba yangu,* "The man whom you saw yesterday is my father."

Note that Swahili uses object prefixes together with the relative particles. In the above sentence, the object prefix *m* "him, her" , (in *uliye-m-wona)* has been used together with *ye.* You certainly remember that *w* has been added to make mw because the verb begins with a vowel, i.e. *ona*, "see". In the plural, this sentence would read:

Watu uliowaona jana ni baba zangu, "The people you saw yesterday are my fathers".

b. With the rest of the classes, the relatives are denoted as follows:

M/MI:	*Mti ulioanguka*, The tree which fell.
	Miti iliyoanguka, Trees which fell.
KI/VI:	*Kitabu ulichonipa*, The book you gave me.
	Vitabu ulivyonipa, The books you gave me.
N:	*Nyumba aliyojenga*, The house he built.
	Nyumba alizojenga, The houses which he built.
MA:	*Tunda lililoiva*, The fruit which is ripe.
	Matunda yaliyoiva, The fruits which are ripe.
	Uso uliotakata, The face which is clean.
	Nyuso zilizotakata, The faces which are clean.
PA:	*Pahali palipochafuka*. The place which is dirty.
KU:	*Kusoma kunakofaa*. Reading which is useful.

Briefly, from the above examples we get the following relative particles for all the noun classes:

MI/WA : *ye* and o	KI/VI: *cho* and *vyo*
M/MI: *o* and *yo*	N: *yo* and *zo*
MA: *lo* and *yo*	U: *o* and *zo*
KU: *ko*	PA : *po* and *zo*

The second way of rendering the relative pronouns is to attach the relative particles to the word *amba*, thus:

mtu amba*ye*...	kitabu amba*cho*...
watu amba*o*...	vitabu amba*vyo*...
mti amba*o*...	nyumba amba*yo*...
miti amba*yo*...	nyumba amba*zo*...

tunda amba*lo*...	uso amba*o*...
matunda amba*yo*...	nyuso amba*zo*...
kusoma amba*ko*...	pahali amba*po*...

Originally Swahili relatives were expressed only by adding the relative particle to the verb. Adding the relative particle to the word *amba* to express relationship is a recent introduction into the Swahili language. It is, nevertheless, accepted as correct Swahili usage.

The relative of time is expressed by *-po-*, "when" e.g.

Alipokuja nilikuwa shuleni,	"When he came I was at school."
Ninaposoma sitaki kelele,	"When I am reading I do not like noise".

In the future tense, the relative particle *kapo* is used, e.g.

Utakapokuja...	"When you come".
Utakapokuja utakuta kazi tayari,	"When you (will) come you will find the work ready".

The relative of place is *ko*, "where", e.g.

Sijui alikoweka kitabu kile,	"I do not know where he put that book".
Je, unajua alikokwenda?	"Do you know where he went?"

Note that *mo* and *po* are also used instead of *ko* with some difference:

Usiingie chumbani walimo wageni.	"Do not enter the room where the guests are".
Palipokaa/walipokaa wazee hakuna cha kuogopa.	"Where old men are (sitting) there is nothing to be afraid of".

EXERCISE 32

Fill in the right relative particles:

1. Wali... kuwa watoto walipenda sana kucheza.
2. Miti ili... anguka jana ilikuwa mirefu sana.
3. Mwizi ali... iba shuleni amekamatwa na polisi.
4. Pahali tuna... kaa ni pazuri sana.
5. Nili... mwona sikumjua, nilifikiri ni mgeni.
6. Watoto wasikae mahali wali... kaa wazee, si vizuri.
7. Mwalimu wetu anapenda nyuso zili... takata.
8. Sijui ana.. weka vitabu vyake, njoo tutafute.

EXERCISE 33

Translate into Swahili:

1. The book which gave me is very nice.
2. Whose book is lost, mine or the teacher's?
3. The man who gave you that book is my father.
4. The house which you see was built by those people.
5. The name which you gave to your dog is not nice.
6. I like to see faces which are clean.
7. Our teacher does not like to see feet that are dirty.
8. The trees which they cut were not theirs.
9. Do not sit on a place which is not clean.
10. Do not eat fruits which are not ripe.
11. Do not read books that are bad, read good books.
12. I like reading which is useful.
13. The thief who stole our clothes is that one.
14. Come tomorrow, you will see the man you want.
15. Do not come tomorrow, you will not see the man you want.

EXERCISE 34

Study this conversation and then translate into English:

Tatu Hujambo, Amina?

Amina Sijambo, habari gani ?

Tatu Nzuri sana, habari za watoto?

Amina Nzuri tu. Unakwenda wapi?

Tatu Nakwenda shuleni kumwona mwalimu aliyekuja jana.

Amina Ndiyo, nimesikia kuna mwalimu aliyekuja jana.

Tatu Twende basi tukamwone, nasikia ni kijana sana.

Amina Nimesikia ni msichana aliyefaulu mwaka huu.

Tatu Watu waliotoka mbali wamekwisha fika shuleni kumpokea mwalimu mgeni. Twende, bwana!

Amina Ngoja nivae viatu vyangu vile virefu.

Tatu Usikawie sana, sipendi kuwa mtu wa mwisho.

Amina Haya, twende dada, tupite njia hii ndiyo fupi.

LESSON 26

SWAHILI ADVERBS AND PREPOSITIONS

ADVERBS OF TIME

juzi, the day before yesterday
jana, yesterday
*kesho, t*omorrow
keshokutwa, the day after tomorrow
usiku, at night
mchana, in daytime
asubuhi, in the morning
jioni, in the evening
zamani, formerly
zamani sana, a long time ago
mapema, early

sasa, now
kila siku, every day
sasa hivi, just now
siku zote, always
bado not yet
bado kidogo, yet a little while
baadaye, afterwards
kwanza, at first
mwishowe, in the end
mwanzoni, in the beginning
usiku wa manane, in the dead of night

ADVERBS OF PLACE

chini, on the ground — e.g. *shuka chini*, come down
juu, above — *juu angani*, in the air; *ruka, juu,* jump up
mbele, in front — *yuko mbel*e, he is in front
nyuma, behind — *yuko nyuma*, he is behind
mbele ya nyumba, in front of the house
nyuma ya nyumba, behind the house

mbele yangu, in front of me

So too with *-yako, yake* etc. (refer Lesson Twenty)

ndani, inside	*wako ndani,* they are inside
nje, outside	*yuko nje,* he is outside
katikati, in the centre	*hapa ni katikati,* here is the centre/middle
karibu, near	*yuko karibu,* he is near
mbali, far away	*wako mbali sana,* they are far away
hapa,	here
hapahapa,	right here
pale,	there
palepale,	on the spot
huko,	there
huku na huko,	here and there
popote,	everywhere/anywhere
kokote,	everywhere/anywhere

ADVERBS OF MANNER

bure, in vain, gratis	*sawasawa*, evenly, O.K.
hakika, certainly	*mbalimbali*, different (ly)
halisi, that's it	*pamoja,* together
hasa, especially	*moja moja*, one by one
hata kidogo, not at all	*zaidi,* more
ghafla, suddenly	*tu,* only
kabisa, indeed	*hivi,* thus
kamwe, not, never	*hivyo,* in that way
kidogo, a little	*vilevile,* also
labda, perhaps	*pia*, also

mno, too much	*lakini,* but
ovyo, disorderly	*naam,* yes/ok
polepole, slowly	*ndiyo,* yes
upesi, quickly	*hapana,* no
haraka, quickly/fast	*siyo,* no
vibaya, badly	*vingine,* otherwise
vizuri, well	*vyovyote,* anyhow
vigumu, hardly	*kiume,* manly

NB Adverbs can also be formed by prefixing *ki* to nouns, thus: *kiungwana,* "like a gentleman" in the manner of a gentleman".

Useful Expressions

Fanya hivi,	Do (it) this way.
Usifanye hivi,	Do not do (it) in this way.
Sikusema hivi,	I did not say that.
Hivyo ndivyo ulivyosema,	That is what you said.
Fanya vyovyote upendavyo,	Do as you please wish.
Mambo yako hivyo ulivyosikia,	Things as you have heard.
Walisemaje ulipowauliza?	What did they said when you asked them?
Amekwendaje ?	How did he go?
Popote ulipo,	Where ever you may be.
Kokote uendako nitakufuata,	I will follow you wherever you go.
Huku na huko,	Here and there.
Palepale,	On the spot.
Hapa hapa,	Right here.
Tazama alivyo,	Look at the way he is.

Tazama nguo zilivyo chafu,	See how dirty the clothes are.
Sikia simba anavyonguruma,	Hear how the lion is roaring.
Hivi ndivyo mambo yalivyo,	That is the way things are.

EXERCISE 35

Insert the right affixes in the blank spaces:

1. Watu hawa ndivyo wali... sema.
2. Je, mmefanya ali... waambia?
3. Tazama mikono ya mtoto ili... michafu !
4. Je, unajua ali... kwenda?
5. Tuli... kuwa watoto tulicheza kila siku.
6. Kitabu kili... potea ni hiki hapa.

PREPOSITIONS

Some adverbs become prepositions when *ya* is added to them, e.g. *baada* ya, from *baada; ndani ya*, from *ndan*i etc..., without changing the sense.

Examples:

Prep.:	*Njoo baada ya kula,*	Come after eating.
Adv. :	*Njoo baadaye,*	Come afterwards.
Prep. :	*Ingia ndani ya nyumba,*	Go inside the house.
Adv. :	*Ingia ndani,*	Go inside.
Prep.:	*Mbele ya shule,*	In front of the school.
Adv. :	*Njoo mbele,*	Come in front.
Prep :	*Nyuma ya shule,*	Behind the school.
Adv. :	*Rudi nyuma,*	Go behind.
Prep.:	*Chini ya meza,*	Under the table.
Adv. :	*Kaa chini,*	Sit down.

Prep. :	*Nje ya nyumba,*	Outside the house.
Adv. :	*Usikae nje usiku,*	Do not stay outside at night.
Prep. :	*Katikati ya mji,*	In the centre of town.
Adv. :	*Kaa katikati,*	Sit in the middle.
Prep. :	*Kati ya shule na shamba,*	Between the school and the farm.
Adv. :	*Weka mpira kati,*	Put the ball in the centre.
Prep. :	*Kabla ya kula,*	Before eating.
Adv. :	*Amekula,*	He has eaten.
Prep. :	*Karibu na,*	Near to.
Adv. :	*Karibu atakuja,*	He is about to come.
Prep. :	*Mbali na shule,*	Far from the school.
Adv. :	*Ameenda mbali,*	He has gone far away.
Prep. :	*Zaidi ya moja,*	More than one.
Adv. :	*Mpe zaidi,*	Give him more.
Prep. :	*Miongoni mwa watu,*	Among the people.
Adv. :	... no adv.	
Prep. :	*Baina ya,...*	Between......
Adv. :	... no adv.	
Prep. :	*Wako pamoja,*	They are together with them.
Adv. :	*Kaeni pamoja.*	Stay together.

LESSON 27

HOW TO TELL TIME IN SWAHILI

The Swahili day begins at 7 a.m. and ends at 6 p.m. It is called *siku* "day". The night is also 12 hours beginning at 7 p.m. and ending at 6 a.m. From 6 a.m. to about 10 a.m. it is *asubuhi,* "morning"; from 11 a.m. to about 4 p.m. it is *mchana,* during the day·; from 5 p.m. to about 8 p.m. it is *jioni,* "evening ". The night is *usiku.* which means also "at night".

e.g. *Alikuja usiku,* "He came at night". Likewise:
Alikuja mchana, "He came during the day".
Alikuja asubuhi, "He came in the morning".
Alikuja jioni, "He came in the evening ".

Swahili time can be reckoned from the English time system in the following manner:

1. From 7 am. to 12 noon: subtract 6 from the English time, and you get the corresponding Swahili time.
   e.g. 7 - 6 = 1 : *saa moja.*
   8 - 6 = 2*: saa mbili.*
   12 - 6 = 6: *saa sita.* etc.

As the word *saa,* " hour" is in the N class, the words *moja, mbili, tatu,* etc. do not take nominal prefixes. We say: *saa tatu, saa nne, saa tano,* etc... Now let us see if you can tell time in Swahili. What time is it in Swahili when it is 9 p.m.? How do you get the Swahili equivalent of 9 p.m.? Of course, you subtract 6 from 9 and get 3; so it becomes *saa tatu usiku* in Swahili.

2. From 1 p.m. to 6 p.m. add 6 to get the Swahili time.
   e.g. 1 p.m. + 6 = 7: *saa saba mchana.*

3 p.m. + 6 = 9: *saa tisa mchana.*
6 p.m. + 6 – 1 2 : *saa kumi na mbili.*

3. Likewise, from 1 a m. to 6 a.m. add 6 to get the Swahili time, thus:
   1 a.m. + 6 = 7: *saa saba usiku.*
   2 a.m. + 6 = 8: sa*a nane usiku.*
   6 a.m. + 6 = 1 2: *saa kumi na mbili asubuhi.*

The expressions *kutwa,* "the whole day", and *kucha,* "the whole night", are common. e.g. *Tulifanya kazi kutwa,* "We worked the whole day". So too, "*Hatukulala usiku kucha,* "We did not sleep the whole night".

EXERCISE 36

Translate into English:

1. Je, ulikuja saa ngapi jana? Nilikuja saa moja jioni.
2. Ni saa ngapi?[18] Sasa ni saa sita mchana.
3. Njoo kesho saa mbili asubuhi, nitakuwa nyumbani.
4. Je, unakwenda kazini saa ngapi? Saa moja na nusu.[19]
5. Je, shule inaanza saa ngapi? Inaanza saa moja.
6. Watoto lazima waende kulala saa moja jioni na waamke saa kumi na mbili asubuhi.
7. Je, siyo mapema mno (too early)? Ni vizuri, watapata afya (health).
8. Tulifanya kazi jana kutwa, tulichoka sana. Tulirudi nyumbani saa tatu usiku.
9. Je, uliamka saa ngapi leo? Niliamka saa kumi na moja.
10. Baba alichelewa kurudi, alikuja saa saba usiku.

---

18 *saa ngapi?* Literally means "how many hours", i.e. "what time is it?"

19 *nusu* means "half", so "half past seven" in this case.

LESSON 28

NOMINAL PREFIXES

SUMMARY

Noun Class	Adjective	Verb		Possessive	Of (-a)
		Aff.	Neg.		
M/WA	m/wa	a/wa	ha/hawa	w/w	w
M/MI	m/mi	u/i	hau/hai	w/y	w/y
KI/VI	ki/vi	ki/vi	haki/havi	ch/vy	chlvy
N	N	i/zi	hai/hazi	y/z	y/z
øMA	Øma	li/ ya	hali/haya	l/ya	l/y
U	m/n	u/zi	hau/kazi	w/z	wiz
PA	pa	pa	hapa	p	P
KU	ku	ku	haku	kw	kw

VERB "TO BE IN A PLACE"

M/WA	yuko/wako (is, are)
MlMI	uko/iko
KI/VI	kiko/viko
N	iko/ziko
MA	liko/yako

U	uko/ziko
PA	pako
KU	kuko
U	uko/ziko

Singular	**Plural**
Mtoto yuko wapi?	Watoto wako wapi?
Mti uko hapa.	Miti iko hapa
Kitabu kiko mezani.	Vitabu viko mezani
Nyumba yako iko wapi?	Nyumba zako ziko wapi?
Yai liko jikoni.	Mayai yako jikoni.
Ufa uko wapi ?	Nyufa ziko wapi?
Pahali pako wapi?	Mahali penu pako wapi?
Kuimba kwake kuko wapi?	Kuimba kwao kuko wapi?

THIS AND THAT

M/WA	huyu/hawa (this, these)	yule/wale (that, these)
M/MI	huu/hii	ule/ile
KI/VI	hiki/hivi	kile/vile
N	hii/hizi	ile/zile
MA	hili/haya	ule/zile
PA	hapa	pale
KU	huku	kule

THAT AND THOSE (near you, or spoken about)

		Singular	**Plural**
M/WA	huyo/hao	mtu huo	watu hao...
M/MI	huo/hiyo	mti huo	miti hiyo...
KI/VI	huyo/hivyo	kitu hicho	vitu hivyo

N	hiyo/hizo	nyumba hiyo	nyumba hizo
MA	hilo/hayo	jina hilo	majina hayo
U	huo/hizo	uso huo	nyuso hizo
PA	hapo	pahali hapo	
KU	huko	kusoma huko	

VERBS: ORDERS AND WISHES

Singular	Plural	Singular	Negative Plural
soma,	*someni,* read	usisome,	*msisome,* don't read
njoo	*njooni,* come[20]	usije	*msije,* don't come
kula	*kuleni,* eat	usile	*msile,* don't eat
nende	*nendeni,* go	usiende	*msiende,* don't go
nije	*tuje,* may I come[20]	usije	*tusije,* may we not come[20]
aje	*waje,* he may come	wasije	*wasije,* they may not

20 As already should this may be translated in various ways, e.g. nije, may mean "may I come? I should come, etc..." depend on the context. Practice alone will enable you to know the right word the right word to use in a given context.

PART TWO

LESSON 29 – 40

LESSON 29

TATU[21] NA WATOTO WAKE NYUMBANI

Vocabulary

nyumbani,	at home
shuleni,	at school
chakula bora,	good, nourishing food
yai, mayai	egg, eggs
maziwa,	milk
mboga,	vegetable
mchele, wali	rice (cooking rice)
matunda,	fruits (sing. *tunda,* fruit)
-bichi,	unripe, uncooked
-bivu,	ripe
kuiva,	to be ripe, to be cooked
safi,	clean
usafi,	cleanliness
chafu,	dirty, dirty
kukataza,	to forbid
karibu na,	near, nearby
mbali ni,	far away from
ugonjwa, magonjwa,	sickness, diseases
japo,	although (also *ijapokuwa, ingawa, ingawaje)*

Tatu ni mama. Ana watoto waTatu Mashaka, Chausiku na Sijali. Tatu anakaa shamba pamoja na watoto wake. Ana shamba la

---

21 In these stories, Tatu appears without a husband; that should not worry you.

matunda na mboga. Tatu anawapa watoto wake chakula bora kila siku: mboga, mayai, matunda, samaki, viazi, mchele/wali, maziwa, nyama, n.k.

Siku moja Tatu alimwona mtoto wake, Mashaka, akila matunda mabichi, akamkataza, kwa sababu si mazuri. Tatu alichukua tunda moja zuri akampa Mashaka. Mtoto huyo alifurahi sana, akasema, "Asante, mama."

Siku nyingine Tatu alikwenda mjini pamoja na mtoto wake, Chausiku. Njiani Chausiku alipata kiu akataka kunywa maji ya mtoni. Mama yake alimkataza akisema, "Maji ya mtoni si safi kwa kunywa, yana vidudu vya magonjwa mbalimbali. Ngoja tufike nyumbani nitakupa maji safi" Japo Chausiku alikuwa na kiu sana hakunywa maji yale, alingoja mpaka walipofika nyumbani. Tatu anawalea watoto wake vizuri; anawafundisha kwa maneno na kwa vitendo pia. Tatu ni mama mwema.

ZOEZI LA 37

1. Je, Tatu ana watoto wangapi? Taja majina yao.
2. Je, Tatu anakaa wapi? Anafanya nini?
3. Je, vyakula gani ni bora?
4. Je, nani alikula matunda mabichi ? Tatu alifanya nini ?
5. Je, mtoto alisema nini alipopewa tunda zuri na Tatu?
6. Je, kwa nini Tatu alimkataza Chausiku kunywa maji ya mto?
7. Je, Chausiku alifanya nini alipokatazwa kunywa maji ya mto na mama yake?
8. Je, Tatu ni mama mwema? Kwa nini unasema hivyo?
9. Je, Tatu alikwenda wapi na Chausiku?
10. Je, maji ya mto ni safi kwa kunywa? Kwa nini?

NYUMBANI : USEFUL EXPRESSIONS

kutandika kitanda,	to make a bed
kupangusa meza,	to dust a table
kuandaa meza,	to set a table
fungua mlango, dirisha,	open the door, the window
funga mlango, dirisha,	shut the door, the window
kufua nguo chafu,	to wash dirty clothes
kupiga pasi nguo,	to iron clothes
kupiga deki,	to wash the floor
weka chakula mezani,	put food on the table
kuona njaa, kiu,	to be hungry, thirsty
kusafisha vyombo,	to wash dishes

HADITHI

Vocabulary

chuma matunda,	pick fruits
jikoni,	in the kitchen
nyani,	a baboon
ogopa	be frightened
mayowe	yells
hodari	brave
fimbo	stick

Tatu alikwenda shambani kuchuma matunda. Alipofika aliona mengine yameiva na mengine hayajaiva. Dada zake, Bahati na Amina, walitaka matunda. Walichuma matunda yote, mabivu na mabichi. Matunda mabichi waliyaweka jikoni yaive, matunda mabivu waliyala palepale. Walikuwa na njaa. Walipokuwa pale shambani alitokea nyani mmoja mkubwa. Tatu na dada zake waliogopa sana. Walikimbilia nyumbani wakilia, "Nyani, nyani! "Waliposikia mayowe hayo, Mashaka na dada zake, Chausiku na Sijali, walitoka nje. Mashaka alikuwa kijana hodari. Alichukua fimbo akaenda shambani kumfukuza nyani yule. Nyani yule alipomwona Mashaka anakuja na fimbo, akakimbia, akaingia porini.

ZOEZI LA 38

1. Je , nani alichuma matunda?
2. Je, matunda yote yalikuwa mabichi ?
3. Je, Tatu na dada zake waliogopa nini? Walifanya nini ?
4. Kwa nini Tatu na dada zake walikula matunda shambani?
5. Je , nani alimfukuza nyani?
6. Je, nyani alikwenda wapi?

AMINA NA MPISHI WAKE JIKONI

Vocabulary

jiko, jikoni,	kitchen, in the kitchen
kijiko, vi-	spoon(s)
umma, nyuma	fork(s)
kisu, vi-	knife, knives
sufuria,	metal cooking pot
sahani,	plate(s)
kikombe, vi-	cup(s)
chai, sukari,kahawa,	tea, coffee sugar
siagi, jibini,	butter, cheese
mkate,	bread
asali,	honey
chumvi,	salt

Amina Mpishi, leo unapika nini?

Mpishi Nitapika wali na samaki, najua wewe huli samaki, nitakupikia nyama.

Amina Vizuri sana, Je, wageni wote wanakula samaki, umewauliza?

Mpishi Hapana, sikuwauliza, ngoja nitakwenda kuwauliza sasa hivi.

Amina Fanya haraka, sasa ni saa tano, tunakula saa ngapi leo?

Mpishi Usiwe na wasiwasi chakula kitakuwa tayari mapema kama kawaida.

Amina Haya nenda, fanya kazi zako, ukitaka msaada niite, unasikia.

Mpishi Ndiyo mama.

CHUMBA CHA KULALA "THE BEDROOM"

Useful Expressions

chumba, vyumba,	room, rooms
chumba cha kulala,	bedroom
kulala,	to sleep, to lie down
kuamka,	to get up, wake up
kuamsha,	to awaken
asubuhi,	morning, in the morning
jioni,	evening, in the evening
mchana,	daytime, during the day
mchana kutwa,	the whole day
usiku,	night, at night
usiku kucha,	the whole night
kitanda, vi-	bed, beds
kitandani,	in the bed, on the bed
mto, mito, pillow(s)	mto, also means "river")
godoro, ma-	mattress (es)
taa, taa ya umeme,	electric lamp
kuwasha taa,	to light a lamp
kuzima taa,	to put out light
choo chooni.	toilet, in toilet
bafu. bafuni.	bath-room, in the bath-room
kuoga,	to take a bath
kunawa,	to wash one's hands and face

LESSON 30

TATU AENDA SOKONI

Vocabulary

soko, sokoni	market, in the market place
mji, mjini,	town, in the town
njia, njiani,	way, on the way
basi, mabasi,	bus, buses
basi, so,	then, enough, stop
kutuma, kutumwa	to send, to be sent
peke yangu, peke yako n.k.	I alone, you alone, etc.
kupenda, kupendana,	to love, to like, to love each other
kukosa; kosa, makosa,	to miss, to make mistake, a mistake, mistakes
nafasi; wakati,	opportunity, time
kuongea,	to talk, converse
kusindikiza,	to accompany, escort
sababu; kwa sababu,	cause, because

Tatu alipokuwa mtoto alikuwa na rafiki jina lake Chenga. Tatu na Chenga walipendana sana. Kila siku walikwenda shuleni pamoja, walicheza pamoja. Siku moja Tatu alitumwa na mama yake sokoni. Njiani alikutana na Chenga, wakaamkiana hivi:

Chenga: Jambo (hujambo) Tatu?

Tatu: Sijambo, je, wewe hujambo?

Chenga: Mimi sijambo kabisa, wewe je?

Tatu: Usiwe na shaka, mimi ni mzima tu.

Chenga: Ni furaha kubwa leo kukutana nawe peke yako saa hizi. Unakwenda wapi?

Tatu: Ninakwenda sokoni, mama amenituma peke yangu leo.

Chenga: Je, nikusindikize? Sina kazi, nitafurahi kwenda nawe.

Tatu: Ukitaka twende, Naogopa kwenda peke yangu.

Chenga: Ni bahati kwangu kupata nafasi hii.

Tatu: Bahati gani? Mbona tunaonana kila siku?

Chenga: Ndiyo, lakini leo ni tofauti na siku nyingine.

Tatu: Tofauti gani? Mimi naona sawa tu kama jana na juzi na siku zote.

Chenga: Iko tofauti , nitakwambia sasa hivi. Twende tu.

Tatu: Haya, niambie basi, kitu gani hicho? Siri, au nini?

Chenga: Usiwe na haraka, nitakwambia tu, ngoja kidogo.

Tatu: Ningoje nini? Niambie tu, niko hapa, sitakukimbia.

Chenga: Nilitaka kukwambia tangu siku nyingi , lakini sikuwa na nafasi.

Tatu: Mbona unazidi kuzunguka tu wala husemi chochote cha maana.

Chenga: Ni hivi, ningependa wewe na mini, tukisha kuwa wakubwa tuoane, unasemaje? Hupendi kuwa mke wangu wa maisha?

Tatu: Maneno yako hayana maana, kama umekosa la kusema heri kunyamaza.

Chenga: Najua huwezi kukubali mara moja, nenda ukafikiri polepole.

Tatu: Sina cha kufikiri, inafaa tuongee mambo mengine. Unaona basi lile?

Chenga: Twende upesi, tutachelewa, mabasi hapa ni shida sana siku hizi.

ZOEZI LA 39

1. Tatu alikutana na nani alipokwenda sokoni?
2. Nani alisema, "Tofauti gani ?"
3. Nani alisema, "Kitu gani hicho?"
4. Nani alimsindikiza Tatu?
5. Nani alisema, "Maneno yako hayana maana?"
6. Nani alisema, "Inafaa tuongee mambo mengine?"
7. Nani alisema, "Ni bahati yangu?"
8. Chenga alimwambia nini Tatu kuhusu kuoana?
9. Je, mabasi ni rahisi au ni shida kuyapata?
10. Je, Tatu alikuwa mtoto au mtu mzima wakati huo?

USEFUL EXPRESSIONS

Bei gani?	What is the price?
Machungwa haya ni thumni kila,	These oranges are fifty cents each
moja na yale pale ni senti thelathini,	and those there are thirty cents each
Nipe matano ya thumni,	Give me five for fifty cents each
Ndizi, je, bei gani?	What is the price of the bananas?
Ndizi ni nne shilingi,	Bananas are four for a shilling
Mbona ghali hivi?	Why are they so dear?
Ndiyo bei yake situ hizi,	This is the price nowadays.
Ebu, nipe nyanya mbili,	Please give two tomatoes
Ni bei gani jumla?	What is the total price?
Nipe shilingi kumi,	Give me ten shillings
Tatu, bado unanunua?	Tatu, are you still buying?
Nimemaliza, twende,	I am ready, lets go.
Vitu vimepanda bei!	Things have become so expensive!
Ndugu yangu, sijui tutafanya nini sasa ?	Oh dear, I don't know what we should do now?
Sisi watu wadogo tuna taabu, kweli	We people of low income are in trouble, indeed!
Basi lile, linakuja,	There comes the bus.
Kwa heri, dada,	Bye bye, dear sister

LESSON 31

DUKANI

Vocabulary

duka ma-,	shop, shops
madukani,	at the shopping centre
kwenda dukani,	to go shopping, to go to the shop
kuuza; kununua,	to sell, to buy
nguo,	clothes, cloth, dress, dresses
nguo mpya nguo ya zamani,	new close, old dress
kushona; cherehani,	to sew, sewing machine
kupima nguo,	to take measure of a dress
nipime nguo,	take my measure of a dress
mashono bei gani?	how much do you charge for sewing?
inategemea kitambaa	it all depends on the material
suruali, koti,	a pair of trousers; a coat
blauzi; sketi	blouse, skirt
sweta,· chupi, vesti,	sweater, underpants, vest
taulo; shuka; mashuka,	towel; bedsheet; bedsheets
blanketi; nguo za watoto,	blanket(s); children's clothes
binzari; pilipili,	curry powder; pepper

Tatu aliwaambia watoto wake waende dukani kununua vitu. Chausiku alisema, "Mama nitakwenda peke yangu dukani siogopi kitu". Mashaka aliposikia vile alifurahi kwa sababu hakutaka kwenda dukani ; alitaka kucheza mpira. Basi , Chausiku aliondoka mara moja. Alifika dukani akakuta watu wengi. Aliuliza, "Je, mchele uko?" Mwenye duka alijibu," Mchele uko, dada; unataka kiasi gani?" Chausiku alijibu, "Nipe kilo tano. Nipe pia nusu kilo ya binzari, robo kilo ya pilipili na kilo moja viazi. Nipe upesi nikimbie nyumbani, mama ananingojea njiani kwa sababu usiku umeingia nami niko peke yangu."Mwenye duka alisema, "Haya, dada Chausiku, vitu vyako hivi hapa, nipe shilingi kumi na thumni. Chausiku alisema, "Sina shilingi kumi na thumni", ninazo shilingi tisa na thumni tu. "Mwenye duka alisema, "Haya, si kitu, nipe hizohizo tu. "Chausiku alitoa fedha, akachukua vitu vyake, akaondoka mbio. Alifika nyumbani kabla giza halijazidi.

ZOEZI LA 40

1. Tatu aliwaambia nini watoto wake?
2. Nani alikwenda dukani?
3. Kwa nini Mashaka hakutaka kwenda dukani?
4. Chausiku alinunua nini na nini dukani?
5. Mwenye duka alitaka shilingi ngapi? Alipata shilingi ngapi?
6. Je, Chausiku alinunua binzari kilo ngapi?
7. Je, nani alisema, "Lete hizohizo tu?"
8. Je, Chausiku alifika nyumbani lini?
9. Je, Chausiku alikwenda dukani na nani?
10. Je, Chausiku aliogopa kwenda peke yake?

Useful Expressions

Dukani; madukani,	In, at the shop(s); shopping centre.
Bei; bei gani?	Price; what is the price?
Viatu vimepanda bei,	Prices have gone up.
Punguza bei,	Reduce the price
Ongeza bei, pandisha bei,	Increase the price.
Ndizi hizi bei gani?	What is the price of these bananas?
Samati hizi bei gani?	How much are these fishes?
Samaki mmoja ni shilingi mbili.	They are two shillings each.
Mbona ghali sana?	Why are they so expensive?
Si ghali, ndiyo bei yao,	They are not expensive, that's the price.
Haya, nipe mbili,	Well, give me two.
Usiuze ghali namna hii.	Don't sell at such a high price.
Nisipofanya hivyo sipati faida	If I don't do that I will get no profit.

LESSON 32

BARABARANI

Vocabulary

mume (wa),	husband, (her)
lami,	tarmac
dereva,	driver
barabara, barabarani,	road, on the road
gari; magari,	car, cars
kuendesha,	to drive
kusimama; kusimamisha,	to stop, to make stop
kukimbiza gari.	drive fast
tope, matope	mud
utelezi, kuteleza,	slippery, to slip
mvua,	rain, to rain
kukwama, kusukuma,	to get stuck, to push
kupanda, kushuka,	to climb up, to descend
kwenda kwa gari,	to go by car

Amina, dada yake Tatu, anafahamu kuendesha gari. Mumewe ana gari jipya aina ya VW. Amina ni dereva hodari, haendeshi mbio, anajua kuwa kukimbiza gari ni hatari. Ukienda kwa gari lake utafurahi, hutaogopa.

Siku moja, Amina alikwenda shambani kwa gari. Njiani aliuliza habari za barabara, kwa sababu mvua ilinyesha usiku. Madereva wengine walimwambia njia ilikuwa mbaya sana, yenye matope mengi na utelezi.

Basi, Amina aliendesha polepole sana, Alikutana na lori moja. Dereva wa lori alikuwa akiendesha mbio. Amina alikwenda pembeni kumpisha, na hapo alikwama vibaya sana. Kwa bahati lori lile lilikuwa na watu wengi wenye nguvu. Walisaidia kusukuma gari la Amina. Alipotoka katika matope, Amina alifurahi sana. Alisema, "Asanteni sana, ndugu. Sijui ningefanya nini peke yangu." Watu wale walimsifu Amina kwa uhodari wake. Walisema, "Dada, wewe ni dereva hodari, lakini barabara hizi hazina dereva hodari, kila dereva hukwama mara kwa mara. Kukwama ni desturi katika barabara zetu kwa sababu hakuna/hazina lami.

ZOEZI LA 41

1. Je, kwa nini Amina alikwama?
2. Je , nani alimsaidia kusukuma gari lake?
3. Je, kwa nini ni desturi kukwama katika barabara zetu?
4. Je, nani alikwenda mbio?
5. Je, nani ni dereva hodari? Amina au dereva wa lori?
6. Je, Amina huendesha mbio? Kwa nini?
7. Je, kwa nini Amina aliuliza habari za barabara?
8. Je, Amina alipata habari gani za barabara?

Useful Expressions

Petroli, stesheni ya petrol,	petrol, petrol station
nipe petroli lita kumni,	give me 10 litres of petrol
hebu, angalia oili,	check the oil
pima upepo,	check the pressure (of tyres)
jaza upepo,	fill in the tyres
kuna pancha,	there is a puncture

ziba pancha hii,	fill this puncture
hakuna pancha;	no puncture, valve leakage
valvu inavuja,	
gari limeharibika,	the car is out of order
tengeneza gari,	repair a car
kuegesha gari,	to park a car
pita kushoto, kulia,	keep left, right
njia ina matope sana,	the way is very muddy
nenda polepole,	go slowly
weka cheni, vingine hupiti,	put chains; otherwise you won't pass
ni hatari; kuna hatari,	it is dangerous; there is danger
gari haliwaki; limewaka,	car does not start; it has started
washa gari; zima gari,	start the car; switch off

LESSON 33

TATU BAHARINI

Vocabulary

bahari, baharini,	ocean; in the ocean
kuogelea, kupiga mbizi,	to swim; to dive
kuvua samaki,	to fish
kuzama, kuzamisha,	to sink; to cause to sink
kuelea, meli,	to float; ship
baharia, mwanamaji,	a sailor, seaman
haramia, maharamia,	sea pirate(s)
kuchafuka,	to be angry, e.g. *bahari imechafuka,* "the sea is rough" *Baba amechafuka leo,* "father is angry today."
katika bahari,	in the sea, in the ocean
katikati ya bahari,	in the middle of the ocean
licha,	let alone, not to mention

Siku moja Tatu alikwenda baharini kuogelea. Alikwenda pamoja na watoto wake. Ilikuwa ni mara ya kwanza kwa watoto wake kufika baharini, licha ya kuogelea. Sijali aliogopa kuingia majini, hasa alipoona mawimbi yakipanda na kushuka kwa nguvu. Mashaka alijitupa majini akajaribu kuogelea. Mama yao alimshika Sijali mkono akamchukua polepole mpaka kweye maji mengi. Chausiku na Mashaka walimfuata mama yao nyuma. Tatu aliwaonyesha namna ya kuogelea. Baada ya muda mfupi Tatu na watoto wake walianza kucheza majini bila woga.

Walipochoka kuogelea, Tatu na watoto wake walikwenda kuangalia meli. Siku hiyo, meli nyingi zilifika kutoka nchi mbalimbali zenye kufanya biashara na nchi hii. Meli hizi zilileta bidhaa na kuchukua mazao ya nchi hii kupeleka nchi za nje. Watoto walimwuliza Tatu maswali mengi kuhusu meli na safari zake. Tatu alijibu maswali machache na hapo aliwaambia watoto wake, "Twendeni nyumbani sasa, nitajibu maswali yenu tukifika nyumbani."

ZOEZI LA 42

1. Je, Tatu alikwenda wapi na watoto wake?
2. Je, nani aliogopa kuingia baharini ?
3. Je, Mashaka aliogopa kuingia majini?
4. Je, nani alijaribu kuogelea?
5. Je, Chausiku alifanya nini baharini ?
6. Je, Tatu alipochoka kuogelea alifanya nini ?
7. Je, meli zinakuja kufanya nini?
8. Je, nani aliuliza maswali mengi?
9. Je, Tatu alijibu maswali yote ya watoto wake?
10. Je, nani alishikwa mkono baharini ?

Useful Expressions

maji kupwa; maji kujaa,	low tide; high tide
maji ya chumvi; maji matamu,	salt water; sweet water (not salty)
mvuvi wa samaki, wa-,	fisherman. -men,
kusafiri majini,	to sail
bandari, bandarini,	port; at the port
kutia nanga, nanga.	to lower the anchor; anchor

kung'oa nanga.	to depart (of ship)
homa ya baharini.	sea sickness
meli imezama,	the ship has sunk
wimbi; mawimbi,	wave, waves
je, unajua kuogelea?	can you how to swim?
sijui hata kidogo,	I can't swim at all
nitakufunza kuogelea,	I will teach you how to swim
kuogelea ni mchezo mzuri,	swimming is a very good game
si vigumu kuogelea,	it is not difficult to swim,
unaelea tu,	you just float
jaribu kuogelea hapa,	try to swim here, the water
maji si mengi	is not deep

LESSON 34

TATU SERENGETI

Vocabulary

nyama, nyama mbichi,	meat, raw meat
mnyama, wanyama,	animal, animals
mnyama wa porini, wa-,	wild animals
mbuga ya wanyama,	plain reserved for animal
bustani ya wanyama	zoo
simba,	lion
tembo,	elephant
chui,	leopard
pundamilia,	zebra
fisi,	hyena
swala,	impala
sungura,	hare
kifaru,	rhinoceros
kiboko,	hippo(s)
nyati,	buffalo
nyani,	monkey(s)
nguruwe,	pig
nguruwe mwitu,	wild pig
Mbuni,	ostrich
twiga,	giraffe

Wanyama wa nyumbani	**Domestic animals**
mbwa,	dog
paka,	cat
mbuzi,	goat
kondoo,	sheep
ng'ombe,	cow, cattle
kuku,	chicken
punda,	donkey
farasi,	horse

Tanzania kuna mbuga kubwa ya wanyama wa porini. Je, unajua jina la mbuga hiyo! Inaitwa Serengeti. Iko karibu na mji wa Arusha. Serengeti kuna wanyama wa kila aina, wakubwa na wadogo, kwa mfano: tembo, twiga, kifaru, simba, chui, nyati, mbuni, swala, na wengine wengi. Ukitaka kuwaona wanyama wote hawa nenda Serengeti. Kila mwaka watu wengi huja Serengeti kuona wanyama. Wanatoka nchi mbalimbali: Ulaya, Marekani, Asia, na nchi nyingine. Tatu na watoto wake walisikia habari za Serengeti. Siku moja, walikwenda kuona wanyama Serengeti. Walipofika Arusha, walikutana na watalii wengi, wakaenda Serengeti pamoja. Tatu alifurahi sana kupata nafasi hii kuwaonyesha watoto wake mbuga hii kubwa ya wanyama. Japo walikuwa ndani ya gari, Sijali aliogopa sana alipoona simba amelala na twiga wakila majani. Mama yake alimwambia, "Usiogope, hakuna hatari." Mashaka na Chausiku waliongea peke yao, sijui waliongea nini. Nafikiri waliongea juu ya wanyama wa porini. Hii ilikuwa mara yao ya kwanza kuona wanyama wengi namna hii. Walifurahi sana. Jioni, Tatu na watoto wake walirudi Arusha mjini , wakalala kwa shangazi yao. Watoto wake walieleza mambo waliyoyaona Serengeti. Shangazi yao alifurahi kusikia hadithi zao, mwishowe alisema, "Mimi pia nitakwenda Serengeti mwaka ujao mtakapokwenda, au mnasemaje? Watoto walijibu wote pamoja, "Ndiyo, shangazi, twende pamoja; Serengeti ni kuzuri sana. Ni moja ya maajabu ya dunia, au sivyo mama?" Mama yao alikuwa bafuni; hakusikia walichosema watoto wake. Kama angesikia, bila shaka angekubaliana na watoto wake.

ZOEZI LA 43

1. Je, Serengeti ni nini ? Iko wapi?
2. Je, watu hufika Serengeti kufanya nini?
3. Je, nani aliogopa simba Serengeti?
4. Je, watalii wanaokuja Serengeti hutoka nchi gani?
5. Je, Tatu alikutana na watalii wapi?
6. Je, nani alisema, "Hakuna hatari?" Kwa nini alisema hivyo?
7. Je, Tatu na watoto wake walilala wapi walipotoka Serengeti?
8. Je, shangazi yao alisema nini?
9. Je, nani alisema Serengeti ni moja ya maajabu ya dunia?
10. Je, nani alikuwa bafuni?

USEFUL EXPRESSIONS

Je, umepata kuona simba?	Have you ever seen a lion?
Je, umekwishafika Serengeti?	Have you been to Serengeti?
Bado sijaona simba, wewe je?	I have not yet seen a lion, how about you?
Twende Serengeti tukaone simba,	Let us go to Serengeti to see lions.
Twende Ofisi ya utalii Arusha,	Lets us go to the tourist office in Arusha.

Je, unapenda kuwinda?	Do you like hunting?
Sijui kupiga bunduki,	I don't know how to shoot a gun.
Sipendi kuwinda, ni hatari,	I don't like hunting, it is dangerous.
Ndugu yangu ni mwindaji hodari,	My brother is a good hunter.
Ana shabaha sana,	He/she has a good shot.
Ana leseni ya kuwinda tembo,	He has a permit to hunt elephant.
Siku moja alifukuzwa na tembo lakini haachi kuwinda,	One day he was chased by elephant. but he did not stop hunting.
Siku moja alikutana na simba porini ana kwa ana hakujua bunduki yake ilivyoanguka,	One day he met a lion face toface, he did not know how his gun dropped (from his hand)
Kuwinda kunapunguza, wanyama, ijapokuwa wanazaliana	Hunting reduces the number of animals, even though they reproduce themselves
Zamani dunia iijaa wanyama,	Formerly the earth was full of animals
lakini leo wamebaki wachache tu	But today only afew remain
Nyama ya nguruwe mwitu ni nzuri, lakini nyama ya swala ni nzuri zaidi.	Meat from wild pigs is good, but the meat from impala is better

LESSON 35

BARS AND RESTAURANTS

Useful Expressions

Some people like to take some refreshments after visiting places like Serengeti, so here are some of the expressions you may need:

chai; chai ya rangi	tea, tea without milk
kahawa; kahawa ya rangi	coffee, coffee without milk
maji ya machungwa,	orange squash, orange juice
maziwa moto; baridi,	hot milk, cold
bia moja baridi sana,	one very cold beer
bia moja moto,	one warm beer
soda na barafu,	soda with ice
Leo kuna chakula gani?	What kind of food is there today?
Leo kuna viazi, nyama na matunda,	Today, there are potatoes, meat and fruit
Je, kuna sikilimu?	Is there ice cream?
Je, naweza kupata saladi?	Can I get some salads?
Bila shaka bwana, utapata,	Certainly sir, you will get it
Niletee maji baridi na wiski,	Bring me cold water and whisky.
Wiski pegi ngapi?	How many pegs of whisky (do you want?)
Nipe nusu glasi, ni pegi ngapi?	Give me half a glass, how many pegs is it?
Ebu, niletee karoti kidogo,	Bring me some carrots.
nyama ya kondoo,	mutton

nyama ya ng'ombe,	beef
nyama ya nguruwe,	pork
nyama ya kuku,	chicken
Je, kuna nyama ya kuchoma hapa?	Do you have roast meat here?
Ndiyo, iko, unataka kiasi gani?	Yes, we have, how much do you want?
Je, wanaweka vitunguu na pilipili?	Do they put in onions and pepper?
Ndiyo, kama unataka watakuwekea,	Yes, if you so desire they will put them in.
Je, unakunywa nini?	What do you drink?
Nakunywa "ndovu"[22] *baridi,*	I drink cold ndovu.

22 *Ndovu:* a brand of beer brewed in Tanzania. Other brands are: *Safari, Plisner, Kilimanjaro, Castle, Kibo, Guiness, Serengeti,* etc.

LESSON 36

KIWANJA CHA NDEGE

Vocabulary

kiwanja; kiwanja cha ndege,	plot, ground, airport
ndege; kwenda kwa ndege,	bird, aircraft, plane, to go by air
kuruka kwa ndege,	to fly (by aircraft)
kushuka; kutua,	to descend, to land
kusafiri kwa ndege,	to travel by air
kupima mizigo,	to check
mzigo; mizigo,	load, loads, luggage
sanduku; masanduku,	suitcase(s)
juu ; juu angani,	up, up in the sky
anga; angani,	sky, in the sky
rubani, ma-,	pilot(s)
wafanyakazi wa ndege,	crew
kwenye kiwanja cha ndege,	at the airport
kukaguliwa na polisi,	to be checked by the police
kuteka nyara ndege,	to hijack plane

Tatu alikuwa na rafiki, jina lake Wambura. Siku moja Wambura alimwandikia Tatu barua. Katika barua ile alisema, "Salamu, rafiki yangu, nitakuja kwa ndege keshokutwa, tutaonana na kuongea mengi..." Tatu alikwenda kiwanjani kumpokea rafiki yake. Wambura alitoka Nairobi kwa ndege ya asubuhi, waliondoka Nairobi saa mbili na walifika Arusha saa mbili na nusu.

Ndege ilipotua, Wambura alitoka pamoja na wasafiri wengine. Tatu alimpokea mizigo yake na kuiweka katika teksi. Njiani waliongea kwa furaha, mara kwa mara walicheka sana. Dereva wa teksi alifurahi pia kusikiliza mazungumzo yao. Kwa kweli ni furaha kuona watu wanaopendana.

Walipofika nyumbani kwa Tatu, watoto walikuja kumsalimu mgeni. Mashaka alisaidia kuchukua mizigo na Chausiku aliandaa meza. Sijali alikuwa nje akicheza na wenzake. Mama yake alimwita, akaja mara moja. Jioni Wambura aliwasimulia habari za safari yake ya ndege.

ZOEZI LA 44

1. Je, rafiki ya Tatu ni nani? Anakaa wapi?
2. Je, barua ilitoka kwa nani? Ilisema nini?
3. Je, rafiki ya Tatu alifika Arusha saa ngapi?
4. Ndege ilichukua muda gani kutoka Nairobi mpaka Arusha?
5. Je, kwa nini dereva wa teksi alifurahi?
6. Je, Sijali alikuwa wapi mama yake alipomwita?
7. Je, nani alisaidia kuchukua mizigo?
8. Je, Chausiku alifanya nini?
9. Je, nani alisafiri kwa ndege na baadaye kusimulia juu ya safari yake?
10. Je, ndege ilipotua Wambura alifanya nini?

Useful Expressions

barua ya ndege,	airmail.
kupeleka barua kwa ndege,	To send letters by airmail.

kuondoka; ndege imeondoka,	To depart, the aircraft has taken off
kupokea mgeni,	to receive a guest.
mgeni alipokelewa vizuri sana,	The guest was very well received.
kusindikiza mgeni,	To see a guest off, to escort.
kuaga; kuagana.	To take leave off, to part company.
ndege kuanguka,	Air crash.
ajali ya ndege,	Air accident.
Barua ya ndege inachukua saa moja toka Arusha mpaka Nairobi,	Airmail takes one hour from Arusha to Nairobi.
kufunga mkanda; kufungua mkanda,	To tie the belt, to untie the belt.
kuvuta sigareti,	to smoke.
Msivute mpaka tufike angani	Don't smoke until we are up in the air.
Zimeni sigara zenu sasa,	Put off your cigarattes now.
Mnaweza kuvuta sasa,	You may smoke now.
Kaeni wima vitini,	Stay up right in your chairs.
Mnaweza kulala sasa,	You may recline now.
Je, hupendi safari ya ndege?	Don't you like to go by air?
Ninaogopa kusaftri angani,	I am afraid to travel in the air.
Hakuna sababu ya kuogopa,	No reason to be afraid.

Ndege karibu itaondoka,	The aircraft is about to take off.
Hali ya hewa si nzuri,	The weather is not good.
Kuna mawingu na ukungu mwingi,	There are clouds and much fog.
Kiwanja kimetanda ukungu,	The airport is covered with fog.
Kuna mvua pia leo,	There is rain also today.
Ndege nyingi zinashindwa kutua shauri ya ukungu,	Many aircraft cannot land because of fog.
Karibu jua litatoka,	The sun is about to come out.
Ukungu umezidi siku hizi,	There is too much fog nowadays.

HADITHI

Ndege moja ilikuwa angani. Rubani aliwaambia wasafiri, "Mnaweza kuvuta sigara sasa." Baada ya muda mfupi, alitoa sauti kubwa akisema, "Zimeni sigara zenu upesi, na fungeni mikanda mara moja." Watu wote waliogopa. Ndege ilikuwa juu ya mawingu, ikaanza kushuka upesiupesi. Chini ya mawingu kulikuwa na ukungu; rubani hakuweza kuona kiwanja cha ndege. Alijaribu kuzunguka, lakini ndege ilizidi kushuka. Mwishowe, alitua shambani. Rubani huyo alikuwa hodari sana. Japo ndege ilikuwa mbovu, lakini alitua salama, hakuna mtu aliyeumia. Ndege ilipotua, wasafiri wote walitoka wakitetemeka. Wote walimshika rubani mkono na kumpa heko kwa uhodari wake. Watu wengi walikuja kuona ajali hii ya ndege. Walishangaa walipoona wasafiri wote salama kabisa. Baada ya saa moja hivi, helikopta ilikuja ikawachukua wasafiri wote.

ZOEZI LA 45

1. Kwa nini rubani alipewa heko na wasafiri?
2. Je, ndege ilitua wapi? Kwa nini ?
3. Je, nani aliyeumia katika ndege hii?
4. Je, kwa nini watu walishangaa?
5. Je, nani alikuja kuwachukua wasafiri?

LESSON 37

KAZINI

Vocabulary

kazi; kazini,	work, at work
kufanya kazi; kwa bidii	to work with effort
kufika kazini,	to report for work
kuchelewa kazini,	to come late to work
kuacha kazi,	to stop working, to resign
kufukuzwa kazi,	to be fired
lazima kila mtu afanye kazi,	everybody must work
mvivu wa kazi,	too lazy to work
hodari wa kazi,	hardworking
kutafuta kazi;	to look for work
kupata kazi,	to get a job
unataka kazi gani?	what type of the work do you want?
Kazi yoyote ile,	any kind of work, no matter what kind
Kulima, kupanda mbegu,	to cultivate, to sow seeds
Kuvuna mavuno,	to harvest, harvest

Tatu ana shamba kubwa. Anafanya kazi shambani pamoja na watoto wake. Kila mwaka wanapanda mbegu nzuri za mahindi, mpunga, maharage na mihogo. Tatu hapendi mtoto mvivu. Siku moja, Mashaka alichelewa kufika shambani. Mama yake alimwambia, "Ukichelewa tena utalima peke yako wakati sisi tumekwenda nyumbani." Toka siku ile, Mashaka hajachelewa tena kazini. Watoto wa Tatu wanajua lazima kila mtu afanye kazi. Tatu anafanya kazi kwa bidii, na watoto wake pia wanafanya kazi kwa bidii. Mwaka jana Tatu na watoto wake walipata mavuno mazuri sana. Tatu hana shida ya chakula, watoto wake kila siku wanakula chakula bora. Mara kwa mara Tatu huenda sokoni kununua samaki, vitunguu na nyama. Kila siku anawapa watoto wake chakula cha kuchukua shuleni. Jioni wakirudi, wanamsaidia kazi shambani. Mashaka ni hodari sana shuleni. Walimu wake wanampenda sana. Chausiku ameanza kusoma juzi tu. Sijali bado mdogo.

ZOEZI LA 46

1. Nani alichelewa kazini siku moja? Tatu alisema nini?
2. Tatu ana nini? Anafanya kazi na nani?
3. Nani alipata mavuno mazuri mwaka jana?
4. Je, kuna shida ya chakula kwa Tatu? Kwa nini?
5. Je, watoto wa Tatu huchukua nini waendapo shuleni?
6. Je, watoto wa Tatu hufanya nini wakirudi nyumbani?
7. Je, kwa nini Mashaka anapendwa na walimu wake?
8. Je, Sijali anakwenda shule? Kwa nini?
9. Je, Chausiku alianza shule lini?
10. Je, nani anafanya kazi kwa bidii?

Useful Expressions

kumaliza kazi,	to finish work
kwenda kazini,	to go to work
kutoka kazini,	to come back from work
baba yuko kazini,	father is at work
baba hajarudi kazini,	father has not yet returned from work
kuanza kazi,	to begin working, to start
kufanya uzembe kazini,	to be careless at work
kuwahi kazini; kuchelewa,	to be on time for work, kuchelewa
kupoteza; kupoteza muda,	to lose; to waste time

SHAIRI LA KUSIFU KAZI

Vocabulary

Shairi, poem	*kusifu,* to praise
karani, clerk	*kupanda,* to plant
us'ende (usiende), do not go	*adhuhuri,* midday
ngazi, step, or staircase	*mnazi,* coconut tree

(**NB** See also the vocabulary list at the end of this book)

1. Usende mjini kutafuta kazi ,
   Utapoteza muda hiyo ni wazi ,
   Kilimo shambani ndiyo hasa ngazi,
   Ya maisha bora hata kiangazi,

2. Ukitaka chakula bora shambani,
   Matunda, mayai , huko ni nyumbani,
   Asubuhi chai , mayai kinywani,
   Mchana nyama, viazi , wali jioni.

3. Utu, maisha mema, na ujirani,
Yamejenga huko bila kisirani,
Hukai peke daima asilani,
Ndugu, jirani mwaishi furahani.

4. Mjini watu hawana ujirani,
Hawajuani tarishi na karani,
Hamuna jambo wapitana njiani,
Hekaheka waenda mbio kazini.

5. Imewatawala fedha mpaka ndani,
Wakikosa hamuna raha nyumbani,
Usingizi hawapati kitandani,
Watafika mpaka huko kiwandani.

6. Nawe shika shauri kaa shambani,
Jenga nyumba yako nzuri ya thamani,
Utapata mwana umwite Shabani,
Uishi vema uwe kwako nyumbani.

(for explanation of the poem see the key)

LESSON 38

SHULE YETU

Vocabulary

shule, shuleni,	school, at school
kusoma; kusomea,	to read, to read for/to
kuandika; kuandikia,	to write, to write to/for
kujenga; kujengea,	to build, to build for/with
darasa. ma-.	classroom(s)
mwanafunzi. wanafunzi.	pupil, pupils
mvulana; wa-	boy(s)
msichana. wa-.	girl(s)
mstari. mi-.	line(s)
kagua. ku-.	to inspect
simama. ku-	to stand up, stop moving
nywele; nywele,	hair, clean hair
nguo; nguo chafu,	dress ; dirty clothes
shule ya msingi.	primary school
shule ya sekondari.	secondary school
chuo kikuu,	university
chuo cha elimu,	college of education
kifaa, vifaa,	equipment, materials

Shule yetu iko katika kijiji. Kijiji chetu kina watu wengi na wengi wao wana watoto. Katika kijiji chetu kila mtoto anakwenda shule. Shule yetu ina wavulana na wasichana wengi, lakini wavulana ni wengi zaidi ya wasichana. Wako wasichana mia mbili na sitini, na wavulana ni mara mbili yao. Je, wako wavulana wangapi? Bila shaka wavulana ni mia tano na ishirini. Jumla ya watoto wa shule yetu ni mia saba na themanini.

Kuna walimu wengi pia, wa kike na wa kiume. Walimu wanaume ni mara tatu ya walimu wanawake. Dada yangu ni mwalimu katika shule yetu. Mwaka jana alikuwa mwalimu mkuu. Mwaka huu amekataa kuwa mwalimu mkuu, anasema ni kazi kubwa mno, hapati nafasi ya kuwatunza watoto wake nyumbani. Watu wengi wanafikiri inafaa wanaume tu wawe walimu wakuu kwa sababu wana nafasi zaidi kuliko wanawake, hasa wanawake wenye watoto wadogo. Mwalimu mkuu wa shule yetu ni hodari sana. Watoto wote na walimu wanampenda. Siku moja, aliwaambia watoto wote walete mawe ya kujengea darasa la saba. Watoto walileta mawe mengi. Mwalimu mkuu pia alileta mawe kila siku asubuhi. Watoto waliweka mawe yao pamoja. Baadaye walisimarna mstarini, mwalimu mkuu akawakagua kuona kama nywele, mikono, miguu na nguo zao ni safi. Wale ambao walikuwa wachafu wakaadhibiwa.

Watoto wachache wanakwenda shule ya sekondari kila mwaka toka shule yetu. Tuna watoto watatu tu wanaosoma Chuo Kikuu cha Dar es Salaam, na watano katika Chuo cha Elimu cha Morogoro, karibu na Dar es Salaam. Walimu wetu wanafanya bidii katika kazi yao ngumu ya kuwafundisha watoto wetu maarifa mbalimbali.

Mbele ya shule kuna shamba kubwa ambalo hulimwa na walimu na wanafunzi. Kila mwaka wanapanda mbegu mbalimbali na wanapata mavuno mazuri. Shule yetu haina shida ya fedha ya kununulia vifaa vya shule. Sisi wazazi pia tunasaidia katika kazi ya shamba la shule. Kuna ushirikiano[23] mzuri kati ya shule na kijiji.

---

23 Ushirikiano here means good relationship, co-operation, understanding. In question 10 (Exercise 47) the world relationship (or *uhusiano* in Swahili) refers to *ushirikiano* (you can lookup the rest of the vocabulary at the back).

ZOEZI LA 47

1. Je, shule yetu ina wasichana wangapi?
2. Je, nani alikuwa mwalimu mkuu mwaka jana?
3. Je, watu wengi wanafikiri nani anafaa kuwa mwalimu mkuu? Kwa nini?
4. Je , kwa nini ni vigumu kwa wanawake kuwa walimu wakuu?
5. Je, kwa nini watoto huleta mawe?
6. Je, kwa nini wanafunzi husimama mstarini mbele ya shule kila siku?
7. Je, mtoto mchafu hufanyiwa nini?
8. Je, watoto wangapi wa shule yetu wanasoma Chuo Kikuu cha Dar es Salaam?
9. Je, kwa nini shule yetu haina shida ya fedha za kununulia vifaa?
10. Je, kuna uhusiano gani kati ya shule na kijiji chetu?

CONVERSATION

Useful Expressions

kwenda shuleni,	to go to school.
kurudi toka shuleni,	to come back from school.
mwalimu yuko shuleni,	the teacher is at school.
hayuko shuleni,	he is not at school.
kusoma shule ya msingi,	to attend primary school
kufanya mitihani,	to do examinations
kufaulu, kushindwa mtihani,	to pass, to fail an examination.
mtihani mgumu, rahisi,	difficult, easy examination.
kupata nafasi,	to have time for. have a chance.
sina nafasi; kwa leo,	I have no time today.
kazi ya kilimo,	agricultural work.
fedha ya kununulia vifaa	money for buying school equipment

TATU TALKS WITH HER SON, MASHAKA

Tatu Je, mtihani ulikuwa mgumu?

Mashaka Ndiyo, mtihani ulikuwa mgumu sana.

Tatu Je, unafikiri utafaulu?

Mashaka Sijui, lakini nilifanya karibu maswali yote.

Tatu Je, watoto wote waliona mtihani ni mgumu?

Mashaka Ndiyo, kila mtoto alisema mtihani huu ni mgumu sana.

Tatu Mwalimu wenu amesemaje juu ya mtihani?

Mashaka	Hakusema neno. Alisema tu "Poleni watoto!"
Tatu	Majibu yatatoka lini?
Mashaka	Majibu yatatoka mwezi ujao.
Tatu	Ukifaulu utakwenda wapi?
Mashaka	Nikifaulu, mama, nitakwenda shule ya sekandari.
Tatu	Je, unataka kusomea nini? Unataka kazi gani?
Mashaka	Ninataka kuwa daktari ili niwatibu wagonjwa. Nchi yetu haina waganga wa kutosha, na wagonjwa ni wengi sana.
Tatu	Vizuri sana, mwanangu, ukiwa mganga nitafurahi sana.

LESSON 39

SIASA YA TANZANIA

Vocabulary

siasa; mwanasiasa; wanasiasa,	politics, politicians
kutawala; utawala	to rule, govern; administration
zamani sana,	a long time ago
Mwarabu; Waarabu,	Arab(s)
Mwajemi; Waajemi,	Persian(s)
Mhindi, Wahindi,	Indian(s)
Mzungu ; Wazungu,	European(s)
Mchina; Wachina,	Chinese
pwani,	coast, at the coast
kwa ajili ya biashara,	on the account of business, trade
utumwa; mtumwa, wa-,	slavery, slave(s)
kukamata, watumwa,	to capture slaves
biashara ya watumwa,	slave trade
ukoloni; ubeberu,	colonialism, imperialism
kiongozi, viongozi,	leader(s)
uhuru; uhuru na kazini,	freedom, freedom and work
Afrika Mashariki,	East Africa
ujamaa; kujitegemea,	socialism, self-reliance
chama; vyama,	association(s), partie(s)
kupigania,	to fight for

Tanzania ni nchi kubwa; iko Afrika Mashariki. Zamani sana Waajemi, Waarabu, Wahindi na baadaye Wazungu walifika pwani ya Tanganyika kufanya biashara. Waarabu walikamata watumwa, walifanya biashara ya watumwa. Wazungu walileta ukoloni na ubeberu Tanganyika

Watanzania walipigania uhuru wao. Leo Tanzania ni nchi huru. Viongozi wanasema kila mara "Uhuru na kazi!" Kila mtu ni lazima afanye kazi. Siasa ya ujamaa na kujitegemea ni siasa ya kazi. Lazima Watanzania wote wafanye kazi kwa bidii wapate kujenga nchi yao. Tanzania ina watu zaidi ya milioni arobaini. lna watoto wengi na wazee wachache. Watoto ni mara mbili ya wazee. Ni lazima watoto wote hawa waende shule kupata elimu. Shule nyingi zimejengwa na wananchi. Chama cha Mapinduzi (C. C. M.) kinachotawala.

Tanzania inaamini kuwa watu wote ni sawa na kinafuata siasa ya usawa wa watu wote, bila kujali tofauti ya rangi , dini, n.k.

Watanzania wote wanajua Kiswahili, lugha ya taifa lao. Watanzania ni wakarimu, na ukifika utafurahia kukaa nao. Ili upate kufurahia safari yako Tanzania, jifunze Kiswahili. Wageni wengi wanaokuja Tanzania wanajifunza Kiswahili; wengi wao wanasema Kiswahili ni lugha rahisi kuliko lugha nyingi duniani. Anza leo kujifunza Kiswahili kwa bidii. Ukitaka kujua Kiswahili safi njoo Tanzania baada ya kumaliza kitabu hiki. Ukifika, jaribu kuongea Kiswahili kila siku bila kuogopa kufanya makosa.

ZOEZI LA 48

1. Tanzania iko wapi?
2. Watanganyika walipigania nini?
3. Waarabu walikuja pwani ya Tanganyika kufanya nini?
4. Je, Tanzania ina watu wangapi?
5. Nani alijenga shule nyingi Tanzania?
6. Je, ukitaka kufurahia safari yako Tanzania ufanye nini?
7. Je, ukitaka kujua Kiswahili safi utakwenda wapi?
8. Je, Tanzania kuna ubaguzi wa dini au rangi?
9. Je, kwa nini ni lazima Watanzania wote wafanye kazi kwa bidii?
10. Je, nani alikuja Tanganyika kwa ajili ya biashara?
11. Je, nani anasema, "Uhuru na kazi"?
12. Je, ukifika Tanzania utafanya nini upate kujua Kiswahili safi?

Political Terminologies

bunge; mbunge, uchaguzi;	parliament, member of parliament; elect
kuchagua,	to choose
kugombea kura,	to campaign for votes
upinzani; mpinzani,	opposition, opponent
kupita bila kupingwa	to be selected without opposition
kura; kupiga kura,	vote, to vote, cast votes
kushinda; kushindwa,	to win, to loose
maendeleo; mapinduzi,	development, revolution
kuendelea,	to develop, to progress

nchi iliyoendelea,	developed country
nchi inayoendelea,	developing country
kunyonya; unyonyaji	to exploit, exploration
kukandamiza, ukandamizaji,	to opresss, oppression
ukombozi; kukomboa,	liberation, to liberate
chama cha ukombozi,	liberation movement
mpigania uhuru, wa-	freedom fighter(s)
kupigania uhuru wa nchi,	to fight for freedom of a country
vita vya ukombozi,	war of liberation
silaha; kuchukua silaha,	arms, to take up arms
zana za vita,	war equipment
bomu;	bomb
mzinga; mizinga,	cannon artillery
bunduki; risasi,	gun, bullet
m*fungwa wa vita, wa -,*	prisoner(s) of war
mkimbizi,	refugee(s)
kambi ya (za) wakimbizi,	refugee camp(s)
kutoa msaada kwa wakimbizi,	to give aid to refugees
kushambulia; kulinda,	to attack; to defend
kushindwa; kushinda,	to be defeated, to win
ushindi; ushindi mkubwa,	victory, big victory
kuunwaga damu,	to spill the blood

LESSON 40

TATU AENDA POSTA

Vocabulary

posta; sanduku la posta	post office, post office box
(SLP)	(P.O. Box)
barua; kuandika barua,	letter, to write a letter
barua ya ndege; kwa ndege,	airmail, by airmail
kupata barua,	to get a letter
kutuma barua,	to send a letter
kuandikiana barua,	to correspond, write each other
kujibu barua,	to answer a letter
stempu; kuweka stempu;	stamp(s) to put a stamp
tarishi, ma-,	messenger(s)
kuchukua, kupeleka,	to take, to send
ngamia; farasi,	camel, horses(s)
treni; basi, kwa miguu,	train, bus, on foot

Tatu alikwenda posta kupeleka barua kwa rafiki yake Wambura. Tatu anakaa Tanzania na Wambwa anakaa Kenya. Tatu na Wambura huandikiana barua mara nyingi. Kila mwaka Tatu na Wambura hukutana mara moja Arusha au Nairobi. Mwaka jana Wambura alikuja Arusha, mwaka huu Tatu atakwenda Nairobi. Kabla ya kwenda ni lazima Tatu atangulize barua kumweleza Wambura siku na saa ya kufika.

Juzi Tatu alipata barua kutoka Nairobi kwa Wambura. Bila kukawia Tatu alijibu mara moja, alisema, "Mpenzi Wambura, salamu sana. Asante kwa barua yako nzuri. Nimefurahi kusikia umefika salama. Pole kwa safari ndefu. Wewe una bahati, unasafiri kwa ndege, mimi bado sijapanda ndege. Kila mara nasafiri kwa basi au kwa treni. Nikipata fedha mwaka huu nitakuja Nairobi kwa ndege. Nitakuarifu mapema uje kunipokea uwanjani..."

Watu wengi wanaandikiana barua siku hizi. Barua zinachukuliwa kwa ndege, kwa treni, kwa basi na hata kwa miguu. Zamani sana huko Uingereza matarishi walikuwa wakipanda farasi kusambaza barua, huko Uarabuni walipanda ngamia, na hapa kwetu walikwenda kwa miguu.

ZOEZI LA 49

1. Je, Tatu anafanya kazi posta?
2. Je, Tatu alikwenda posta kufanya nini?
3. Je, rafiki ya Tatu anakaa wapi? Jina lake nani?
4. Je, Tatu alipata barua lini?
5. Barua zinapelekwaje siku hizi?
6. Je, matarishi wa Uarabuni walipanda nini zamani?
7. Je, matarishi wa wapi walikwenda kwa miguu?
8. Je, nani hajapanda ndege, Tatu au rafiki yake?
9. Je, Tatu atakwenda wapi mwaka huu?
10. Je, Tatu na rafiki yake hukutana kila mwaka mara ngapi?

Useful Expressions

kupeleka simu, kupiga simu,	to send a telegram
Neno moja ni shilingi moja,	one word costs one shilling
kutuma fedha kwa simu,	to send money by telegram
kwa posta,	by postal order
Nataka kupiga simu Nairobi.	I want to call Nairobi

dakika tatu ni shilingi kumi.	Three minutes cost ten shillings
Nipe fomu ya simu.	Give a telegram form.
Jaza fomu hii hapa.	Fill the form here.
Weka sahihi yako hapa,	Sign your name here.
Kuna gundi hapa?	Is there gum here?
bahasha za rejesta.	envelopes for registered letters
karatasi za ndege.	aerogrammes,
Posta kubwa iko wapi?	Where is main post office?
Posta kubwa iko mjini.	It is in town.
Unafikaje mjini toka hapa?	How do you get there (town) from here?
Kuna basi, kituo kile pale.	There is a bus, the bus-stop is there
lnachukua muda gani kufika?	How long does it take to get there?
Nusu saa au zaidi dogo,	Half an hour or a little more.
Nisaidie chenji,	Please, some change.

KEY TO EXERCISES

PART ONE

EXERCISE 1 (Pg. 6)

1. *Karibu.*
2. *Sijambo.*
3. *Nzuri.*
4. Please, sit down. The answer is Asante, or Starehe.
5. *Shikamoo* is used to greet older people and those senior in status. The answer is *Marahaba.*
6. *Karibuni.*
7. *Kwa heri.*
8. *Hodi.*
9. *Pole.*
10. *Asante,* or *nimekwisha poa.*
11. *Hongera.*
12. *Asante.*

EXERCISE 2 (Pg. 9)

1. Pupils, thieves, women, companions, guest, servant
2. Drunkard, wife, husband, director, cook, old man, liar.
3. Man, child, sick person (patient), girl, boy, child, thief.
4. Waongo, wezi, wenzi, wanawake, wanaume, waume, walimu.
5. Wasichana, wanadamu, wazee, wanafunzi, watoto, wageni.

EXERCISE 3 (Pg. 13)

1. Mgeni safi;
2. watu wekundu;
3. walevi wengi

4. wapishi hodari;
5. wagonjwa wachache;
6. watoto weusi;
7. mwalimu mweupe;
8. nice mwema;
9. wanaume hodari;
10. watu wote;
11. baba mkali;
12. wake hodari;
13. wanaume wazito;
14. watoto wafupi;
15. wazee warefu;
16. mgonjwa mwepesi;
17. mwanamke bora;
18. wanafunzi wengi;
19. mpishi mzuri.

EXERCISE 4 (Pg. 14)

1. Wapishi ni waganga hodari na vipofu ni watu wazuri.
2. Wageni ni wanawake wazuri na ni wake hodari.
3. Wazee ni walevi wakubwa na wasichana ni wanawake wadogo.
4. Wezi ni werevu na ni watu waongo na wabaya.
5. Walimu ni watu wema na ni baba wazuri.
6. Watumishi ni watu wafupi na werevu.

EXERCISE 5 (Pg. 14)

1. Mama ni mpishi hodari (wazuri); waganga ni watu wazuri (wema).
2. Wanaume na wanawake ni watu; watoto ni watu wadogo.
3. Watumishi ni watu wazuri; watumishi ni wanawake.
4. Wageni ni watu warefu; wageni ni watu weupe.
5. Tatu ni mke mzuri na Mashaka ni mtoto mzuri.
6. Wanaume wengi ni waume wazuri na wanawake wengi ni wake wazuri.
7. Wanafunzi wengi ni watoto wadogo na walimu wengi ni wazee.
8. Watu wengi ni wagonjwa, watu wachache ni waganga.
9. Wageni wengi ni watu warefu, wachache ni wafupi.
10. Amina ni mwalimu hodari na mama mzuri sana.
11. Vipofu wanaume ni wachache; vipofu wanawake ni wengi.
12. Watoto wote ni weupe na wazee wote ni weusi.

EXERCISE 6 (Pg. 16)

1. Mtoto mdogo ana mikono na miguu midogo.
2. Watu wafupi wana miguu mifupi na watu warefu wana miguu mirefu.
3. Ana moyo mzuri na midomo mizuri.
4. Mwanzo ni mgumu lakini mwisho ni rahisi.
5. Walimu na waganga wana mioyo mizuri.
6. Wagonjwa ni wengi lakini waganga ni wachache.
7. Mitende ni mirefu na ina mizizi mirefu.
8. Mioyo miepesi ni mizuri lakini mioyo mizito ni mizuri pia.
9. Mashaka ana miguu mirefu na mdomo mkubwa.
10. Miaka mirefu ni mingi, lakini miaka mifupi ni michache.
11. Wazee wana miili mizito na miguu miepesi.

EXERCISE 7 (Pg 17)

1. vidole virefu;
2. ana kichwa kikubwa;
3. ana kitanda kirefu; (4) viazi vingi;
4. viatu vizuri sana;
5. wezi wana vifua vipana;
6. visu vikal i;
7. kikapu kikubwa.

EXERCISE 8 (Pg. 18)

1. vitabu vyeusi;
2. viti vyepesi;
3. chumba cheupe;
4. kikombe kidogo;
5. chuma laini;
6. chombo chembamba;
7. mtoto ana viazi vyeupe;
8. watoto wana viazi vyeupe;
9. chakula kidogo;
10. vyakula vidogo;
11. vitu vingi;
12. vyuma vikubwa;
13. viti virefu;
14. visu vikali;
15. viazi ghali;
16. viazi rahisi;
17. kikombe kidogo.

EXERCISE 9 (Pg. 19)

1. nazi tamu;
2. meza kubwa;
3. saa ndefu;
4. faida na hasara;
5. furaha na uchungu;
6. chai na sukari;
7. mkate na nyama;
8. viazi na chumvi;
9. fedha nyingi
10. njia pana;
11. saa chache;
12. kalamu kali;
13. habari nzuri au habari mbaya;
14. chupa nyepesi ;
15. saa ndefu.

EXERCISE 10 (Pg. 23)

1. Mtoto ana macho mazuri na masikio makubwa.
2. Walimu wana macho makali na masikio mapana.
3. Mbwa ana jina zuri.
4. Swali ni gumu lakini jibu ni rahisi.
5. Wazee hujadili mambo muhimu.
6. Wanawake wenye masanduku makubwa wana habari nzuri.
7. Watoto wadogo wana maji na mama wana maziwa.
8. Ndizi na matunda; nyumba na milango; mashamba na majani.
9. Mawe makubwa ni machache, lakini mawe madogo ni mengi.
10. Macho na masikio ni maajabu; mvua na mito pia.

EXERCISE 11 (Pg. 23)

1. Watoto wana mikono midogo na macho makubwa.
2. Wageni ni wengi na wote ni watu wazuri.
3. Viti ni vichache na watoto ni wengi.
4. Ndizi ni matunda matamu na ni mengi.
5. Mikate ni mizuri na ni mingi.
6. Chakula ni ghali lakini ni kidogo.
7. Kiswahili ni lugha nzuri na rahisi.
8. Nyumba ni kubwa, lakini vyumba ni vidogo.
9. Milango ni mipana na mizuri, lakini michache.
10. Wagonjwa ni watu wapole na walimu ni watu bora.

EXERCISE 12 (Pg. 26)

1. Umoja ni nguvu; umoja ni kitu kizuri.
2. Wizi ni mbaya, utu ni bora.
3. Nyimbo ni ndefu lakini tamu.
4. Kuta ni ndefu na pana.
5. Usingizi ni mzuri usiku.
6. Umri mkubwa ni mzuri sana, lakini ujana ni bora.
7. Magonjwa ni mabaya
8. Ulimwengu ni mkubwa na mpana.
9. Unga ni mzuri, lakini mikate ni mibaya.
10. Maua bustanini ni mazuri.

EXERCISE 13 (Pg. 27)

1. Kusoma ni kuzuri, lakini kusoma mno ni kubaya.
2. Hoteli kubwa zina vyumba vingi na vitanda vizuri.
3. Arusha ni pahali pakubwa; pana watu wengi, na usiku kuna kuimba kuzuri na kucheza dansi.

4. Ulimwengu ni pahali pazuri.
5. Kuta ni ngumu.
6. Kula ndizi tu ni tabia mbaya.

EXERCISE 14 (Pg. 31)

1. Watu watano walifika hapa jana.
2. Viti vitatu ni vibovu.
3. Ni ishirini na tisa (29).
4. Ni sita (6).
5. Kumi elfu, mia tano hamsini na tano; mia nne thelathini na mbili; elfu moja mia sita na sabini na nane.
6. Kumi mara kumi na tano ni mia moja na hamsini.
7. Ishirini na moja kujumlisha na sitini ni themanini na moja.
8. Mia tisa na saba kutoa mia sita na sabini na nane baki ni mia mbili ishirini na tisa.

EXERCISE 15 (Pg. 33)

1. Tatu ni msichana mwema kuliko wote hapa, lakini si mrefu kuliko wote.
2. Mashaka ni mkubwa kama wewe, lakini ni mfupi kuliko wewe.
3. Kilimanjaro ni mlima mrefu kuliko yote Afrika.
4. Tanzania ni kubwa kuliko Kenya, lakini Nairobi ni kubwa kuliko Dar es Salaam.
5. Je, New York ndio mji mkubwa kuliko yote duniani?
6. Kujifunza ni bora kuliko kuogelea.

EXERCISE 16 (Pg. 37)

1. The guests have arrived; the cook is cooking plenty of food.
2. Women like flowers ; girls are picking flowers now.
3. The patients are sleeping now; the doctor has gone to see lions and elephants.

EXERCISE 25 (Pg. 67)

1. Je, nani ameona vitabu vya mwalimu leo?
2. Wageni wameleta mizigo yao.
3. Walikuwa na mizigo mingi sana na mizito.
4. Nyumba yetu ni kubwa na nzuri , ina milango miwili.
5. Wape funguo zao, funguo zako ziko wapi ?
6. Majina ya watoto hawa ni magumu, lakini mazuri.
7. Miguu yake ni mizuri kuliko miguu ya dada yake.
8. Kusoma kwake si kuzuri, lakini kuandika kwake ni kuzuri.
9. Mkono wa mtoto mdogo ni mdogo, na kichwa chake ni kidogo pia.
10. Je, umemwona mtoto wangu? Alikuwa na watoto wako.

EXERCISE 26 (Pg. 68)

1. Watoto wake hawaendi shuleni leo.
2. Mwalimu wetu hali shuleni, anakula nyumbani.
3. Je , unakwenda kula wapi? Sili hapa.
4. Mpishi wao haji leo.
5. Mwambie aje keshokutwa.
6. Vitabu vyetu viko wapi ? Nguo zetu ziko wapi ?
7. Nilisikia watu wakipiga makelele: Mwizi huyo ! mwizi huyo !
8. Mtu yule ni nani? Mtu yule ni mgeni wetu.
9. Mtoto wa nani huyu? Mtoto huyu ni wake.
10. Watu wale ni nani? Watu wale ni wageni wetu.
11. Niletee mtoto huyo, ninataka kumwona.
12. Je, niende sasa? Sina kazi. Nenda, na usije tena kunisumbua.

EXERCISE 27 (Pg. 71)

1. If you came yesterday you would have met our guest here.
2. If he gives (you) the money, give him this book.
3. If he does not give (you) the money don't give him this book.
4. If many people want something give it to them.
5. We went to school and found the teacher reading that book.
6. If you don't eat fish they will cook you bananas and meat.
7. Let me tell you about that drunkard.
8. If he had not told me to wait, I would not have waited.

EXERCISE 28 (Pg. 74)

1. Wageni wengi walipokelewa nasi jana.
2. Mwalimu wao anapendwa sana na watoto.
3. Barua nzuri imeandikwa na Bahati kwa wino.
4. Jambo hili limesahauliwa na watu wengi sasa.
5. Wafanyakazi wote wamefikiriwa na waziri.
6. Mlango wa chumba changu umefunguliwa na nani ?
7. Mti ule mrefu ulikatwa na baba kwa shoka.
8. Nyumba ile nzuri ya mwalimu wetu ilivunjwa na wezi usiku.
9. Nguo ya Bahati ilipasuliwa na mbwa kwa makucha yake makali.
10. Watoto walikatazwa na mama wasicheze chumbani.

EXERCISE 29 (Pg. 80)

1. Inafaa ujifunze Kiswahili.
2. Watoto lazima waende shuleni sasa.
3. Je, unafanya nini? Ninajifunza Kiswahili.
4. Inatosha, twende kuona rafiki (also kuwaona marafiki).

5. Lazima nijifunze Kiswahili kila siku, nataka kujua Kiswahili.
6. Inawezekana kujua Kiswahili kwa miezi miwili.
7. Mwalimu wako ni nani? Je, una vitabu vizuri ?
8. Hakuna vitabu vizuri madukani.
9. Mwalimu wetu anakuandikia kitabu.
10. Simjui mwalimu wenu, jina lake ni nani ?
11. Je, unataka kumwona? Njoo kesho utamwona. Anataka kukuona pia
12. Si kitu (haidhuru), si lazima kumwona.
13. Inawezekana kujifunza Kiswahili bila mwalimu.

EXERCISE 30 (Pg. 81)

1. Sukari haipatikani hapa siku hizi.
2. Wezi wamekamatwa na polisi.
3. Kazi hii haiwezekani leo.
4. Macho yake hayaoni vizuri sasa.
5. Je, mtoto wako alizaliwa lini ?
6. Je, unataka sisi tuende wapi kesho?
7. Haifai watoto wacheze shuleni, lazima wajifunze.
8. Je, alisema watumishi wafanye nini ?
9. Je, wageni hawali sasa?
10. Je, ukimwona simba utafanya nini ?
11. Mwambie mpishi aje hapa, nataka anionyeshe chakula cha leo.
12. Mama alisema ninyi mle ndizi kila siku.
13. Mzee alisema nisome barua hii, sijui kusoma.
14. Mgonjwa anasema haji kula leo, mpelekee chakula.
15. Wageni walipokelewa na watoto kwa nyimbo.

EXERCISE 31 (Pg. 83)

1. Mwizi ameonekana mjini.
2. Haiwezekani kwenda sasa, tungoje kidogo.
3. Anajulikana sana na anapendwa na watu wengi.
4. Wanawake uliowaona jana hawapatani.
5. Sijui kwa nini waligombana.
6. Inafaa kuamkiana mnapokutana.
7. Ni vibaya kupigana au kugombana.
8. Tatu aliachana na mume wake, lakini sasa wamerudiana.
9. Hawa watoto wawili wanapendana sana, wanafuatana kila pahali (or popote) nakila siku.
10. Marafiki huandikiana barua ndefu mara nyingi.
11. Funika chakula chako kwa sababu nzi wanapenda chakula chako pia.
12. Nani hutandika kitanda chako kila (siku) asubuhi ?
13. Mvishe mtoto upesi, lazima twende sasa.
14. Kwa nini walimcheka mgeni?
15. Je, unapika nini leo? Sili samaki.

EXERCISE 32 (Pg. 87)

1. Walipokuwa watoto walipenda sana kucheza.
2. Miti iliyoanguka jana ilikuwa mirefu sana.
3. Mwizi aliyeiba shuleni amekamatwa na polisi.
4. Pahali tunapokaa ni pazuri sana.
5. Nilipomwona sikumjua, nilifikiri ni mgeni.
6. Watoto wasikae mahali walipokaa wazee, si vizuri.
7. Mwalimu wetu anapenda nyuso zilizotakata
8. Sijui anakoweka vitabu vyake, njoo tutafute.

EXERCISE 33 (Pg. 87)

1. Kitabu ulichonipa ni kizuri sana.
2. Kitabu cha nani kimepotea, changu au cha mwalimu?
3. Mtu aliyekupa kitabu kile ni baba yangu.
4. Nyumba unayoiona ilijengwa na watu wale.
5. Jina ulilompa mbwa wako si zuri.
6. Napenda kuona nyuso zilizotakata (ambazo ni safi).
7. Mwalimu wetu hapendi kuona miguu michafu (isiyotakata..ambayo ni michafu)[24].
8. Miti waliyokata haikuwa yao.
9. Usikae pahali ambapo si safi.
10. Usile matunda ambayo si mabivu (or ambayo hayakuiva).
11. Usisome vitabu ambavyo ni vibaya, soma vitabu vizuri.
12. Napenda kusoma ambako kunafaa.
13. Mwizi aliyeiba nguo zetu ni yule.
14. Njoo kesho, utamwona mtu unayemtaka.
15. Usije kesho, hutamwona mtu unayemtaka.

EXERCISE 34 (Pg. 88)

Tatu How are you, Amina?

Amina I am well , how are you?

Tatu Quite well, how are the children?

Amina They are well. Where are you going?

---

24 In no. 7, the relative particle, *ambayo*, is omitted. *Miguu michafu* is therefore the same as *miguu ambayo ni michafu*.

Tatu	I am going to school to see the teacher who came yesterday.
Amina	Yes, I heard there is a teacher who came yesterday.
Tatu	Come on, then, let us go to see him, I hear he is very young.
Amina	I hear it is a girl who just graduated this year.
Tatu	People from distant places have already arrived at school to receive the new teacher. Hello, let us go !
Amina	Wait, let me put on my high heeled shoes.
Tatu	Don't be too long, I don't like to be the last person (to arrive).
Amina	Well , let us go, sister; let us take this path, it is a short-cut.

EXERCISE 35 (Pg. 92)

1. Watu hawa ndivyo walivyosema.
2. Je, mmefanya alivyowaambia?
3. Tazama mikono ya mtoto ilivyo michafu!
4. Je, unajua alikokwenda?
5. Tulipokuwa watoto tulicheza kila siku.
6. Kitabu kilichopotea ni hiki hapa.

EXERCISE 36 (Pg. 95)

1. At what time did you come yesterday? I came at 7p.m.
2. What time is it now? It is 12 noon.
3. Come tomorrow a t 8 a.m. , I will be at home.

4. When do you go to work? At 7.30 a.m.
5. When does school begin? It begins at 7 a. m.
6. Children must go to bed at 7 p.m. and wake up at 6 a.m.
7. Is it not too early? It is good, they will be healthy.
8. We worked the whole day yesterday, we were very tired. We returned home at 9 p.m.
9. At what time did you get up today? I got up at 5 a.m.
10. Father came back late; he came at 1 a.m.

PART TWO

LESSON 29

TATU AND HER CHILDREN AT HOME

Tatu is a mother. She has three children: Mashaka, Chausiku and Sijali.Tatu lives in a rural area with her children. She has a garden of fruits and vegetables. Tatu gives her children nutritious food everyday: vegetables, eggs, fruits, fish, potatoes, rice, milk, meat, etc.

One day, Tatu saw her child, Mashaka, eating unripe fruits. She forbade him, for they are not good. Tatu took one good fruit and gave it to Mashaka. That child was very glad and said, "Thank you, mother."

Another day, Tatu went to town with her child, Chausiku. On the way Chausiku felt thirsty and wanted to drink some river water. Her mother forbade her saying, "River water is not good for drinking; it has germs of various diseases. Wait until we get home, I will give you some clean water."

Although Chausiku was very thirsty she did not drink that water; she waited until they reached home. Tatu brings up her children well, she teaches them by words and by deeds also. Tatu is a good mother.

EXERCISE 37 (Pg. 101)

1. How many children has Tatu? Mention their names.
2. Where does Tatu stay? What does she do?
3. Which types of food are nutritious?
4. Who ate unripe fruits? What did Tatu do?
5. What did the child say when he was given a good fruit by Tatu?
6. Why did Tatu forbid Chausiku to drink river water?
7. What did Chausiku do when she was refused by her mother to drink river water?
8. Is Tatu a good mother? Why do you say so?
9. Where did Tatu go with Chausiku?
10. Is river water good for drinking? Why?

A STORY

Tatu went to the garden to pick fruits. When she arrived she saw that some fruits were ripe while others were not. Her sisters, Bahati and Amina, wanted some fruit. They picked all the fruit, the ripe ones and the unripe ones. They put the unripe fruit in the kitchen to ripen. They ate the ripe fruit on the spot. They were hungry. While they were there in the garden, there appeared a big monkey. Tatu and her sisters were very much frightened.

They ran home crying, "Monkey, monkey! "Mashaka and his sisters, Chausiku and Sijali, came out when they heard those yells. Mashaka was a brave young man. He took a stick and went to the garden to chase away the monkey. When that monkey saw Mashaka coming with a stick it ran away and entered the bush.

EXERCISE 38 (Pg. 103)

1. Who picked the fruits?
2. Were all the fruits unripe?
3. What did Tatu and her sisters fear? What did they do?
4. Why did Tatu and her sisters eat fruits in the garden?
5. Who chased away the monkey?
6. Where did the monkey go?

AMINA AND HER COOK IN THE KITCHEN

Amina Cook, what will you cook today?

Cook I will cook rice and fish. I know you don't eat fish; I will cook you some meat.

Amina Very well. Do all the guests eat fish? Did you ask them?

Cook No, I did not ask them; wait, I am going to ask them right away.

Amina Hurry up, it is 11 a.m. When are we going to eat today?

Cook Don't worry, food will soon be ready as usual.

Amina Well, go, do your work; if you need any help, call me, do you hear?

Cook Yes, mother.

LESSON 30

TATU GOES TO THE MARKET

When Tatu was a child she had a friend, his name (was) Chenga. Tatu and Chenga loved each other very much. Every day they went to school together and played together. One day Tatu was sent by her mother to the market. On the way she met Chenga, they greeted each other as follows:

Chenga Hello tatu!

Tatu I am well and how are you?

Chenga I am well, and you?

Tatu I am well (don't worry, I am well).

Chenga I feel so happy to meet you alone at this time (at these hours). Where are you going?

Tatu I am going to the market; mother has sent me alone today.

Chenga May I accompany you? I have no work, I will be glad to go with you.

Tatu If you want, let us go. I am afraid to go alone.

Chenga I am lucky to get this opportunity.

Tatu Why? Don't we see each other every day?

Chenga Yes, but today is different from all other days.

Tatu What is the difference? For me everything is the same as yesterday, the day before yesterday and always.

Chenga There is a difference, I will tell you just now. Let us (just) go.

Tatu Well now , tell me, what is i t? A secret or what?

Chenga Don't be in a hurry, I will tell you, wait a little.

Tatu What should I wait for? Just tell me, I am here, I will not run away from you.

Chenga For a long time I had wanted to tell you, but I did not get a chance.

Tatu Why are you beating about the bush? (going round and round without saying anything concrete).

Chenga It is like this. I would like you to marry me when we are grown ups, what do you say?

Don't you like to be my wife for life?

Tatu Your words make no sense (have no sense); if you have nothing to say better keep quiet.

Chenga I know you cannot agree at once, go and think over it slowly.

Tatu I have nothing to think about, let us speak about something else. Do you see that bus?

Chenga Let us go quickly, we will be late, buses are difficult (to get) here these days.

EXERCISE 39 (Pg. 108)

1. When Tatu was going to the market whom did she meet on the way?
2. Who said, "What difference"?
3. Who said, "What (thing) is that?"
4. Who, accompanied Tatu?
5. Who said, "Your words are meaningless?"
6. Who said, "Let us speak about something else"?
7. Who said, "I am lucky"?
8. What did Chenga tell Tatu concerning marriage?
9. Are buses easy or difficult to get?
10. Was Tatu a child or an adult at this time?

LESSON 31

AT THE SHOP

Tatu told her children to go to the shop to buy things. Chausiku said, "Mother, I will go alone to the shop, I am not afraid of anything. Mashaka was glad to hear that, because he did not like to go to the shop; he wanted to play football. So, Chausiku left at once. She came to the shop and found many people. She asked, "Is there rice?" The shopkeeper answered, "There is rice, sister; how much do you want?" Chausiku answered, "Give me 5 kilos. Give me also half a kilo of curry powder, a quarter kilo of pepper, and a kilo of potatoes. Give me quickly so that I may run home; mother is waiting for me on the way, for it is dusk and I am alone." The shopkeeper said, "Well, sister Chausiku, here are your things, give me Shs. 10/50. Chausiku said, "I haven't 10/50, I have only 9.50". The shopkeeper said, "Well, never mind, give me that only. "Chausiku gave him the money and took her things and left, running. She arrived home before it was too dark.

EXERCISE 40 (Pg. 111)

1. What did Tatu tell her children?
2. Who went to the shop?
3. Why did Mashaka dislike going to the shop?
4. What did Chausiku buy in the shop?
5. How many shillings did the shopkeeper want? How many did he get?
6. How many kilos of curry powder did Chausiku buy?
7. Who said, "Give me that (money) only"?
8. When did Chausiku arrive home?
9. With whom did Chausiku go to the shop?
10. Was Chausiku afraid to go alone?

LESSON 32

ON THE ROAD

Amina, Tatu's sister, knows how to drive a car. Her husband has a new car, a VW model. Amina is an excellent driver, she does not drive fast, she knows that fast driving is dangerous. If you go by her car you will enjoy it, you will not be afraid.

One day, Amina went to the farm by car. On the way there she enquired about the condition of the road, as it had rained the night before. Other drivers told her that the road was very bad, that it had much mud and was slippery. So Amina drove very slowly. She met with one lorry. The driver of the lorry was driving very fast. Amina pulled aside to let him pass, and there upon got stuck very badly. Fortunately, that lorry had many strong men. They helped to push Amina's car. When she got out of the mud, Amina was very glad. She said, "Thank you very much, brothers. I don't know what I would have done." Those men praised Amina for her skill (in driving). They said, "You are a very good driver, sister, but these roads have no good dnver, every driver gets stuck now and then. It is customary to get stuck on these roads of ours, because there is no tarmac."

EXERCISE 41 (Pg. 114)

1. Why was Amina stuck?
2. Who helped her to push her car?
3. Why is it customary to get stuck on our roads?
4. Who drove fast?
5. Who is a good driver? Amina or the lorry driver?
6. Does Amina drive fast? Why?
7. Why did Amina enquire about the condition of the road?
8. What information did Amina get about the road?

LESSON 33

TATU AT THE OCEAN

One day, Tatu went to the ocean to swim. She went with her children. It was the first time for her children to be (reach) at the ocean, let alone to swim. Sijali was afraid of going into the water, especially when she saw waves going up and down violently. Mashaka jumped (threw himself) into the water and tried to swim. Their mother held Sijali by the hand and took her slowly into the deep water. Chausiku and Mashaka followed their mother behind. Tatu showed them how to swim. After a short time, Tatu and her children began to play in the water without any fear.

When they were tired of swimming, Tatu and her children went to see the ships. On that day many ships had arrived from different countries which have business relations with this country. These ships brought goods and took crops from this country to other countries (foreign countries). The children asked Tatu many questions about the ships and their voyages. Tatu answered a few questions and then told her children, "Let us go home now, I will answer your questions when we get home."

EXERCISE 42 (Pg. 117)

1. Where did Tatu go with her children?
2. Who was afraid to go into the water?
3. Was Mashaka afraid of going into the water?
4. Who tried to swim?
5. What did Chausiku do in the ocean?
6. What did Tatu do when she got tired of swimming?
7. What do ships come for?
8. Who asked many questions?
9. Did Tatu answer all the questions of her children?
10. Who was held by the hand in the ocean?

LESSON 34

TATU AT SERENGETI

In Tanzania there is a big park inhabited by wild animals. Do you know the name of this park? It is called Serengeti. It is near the town of Arusha. In Serengeti there are animals of every sort, big and small, for example: elephants, giraffes, rhinoceros, lions, leopards, buffaloes, ostriches, impalas, and many others. If you want to see all these animals go to Serengeti. Every year many people go to Serengeti to see animals. They come from different countries: Europe, America, Asia, and others.

Tatu and her children heard about Serengeti. One day, they went to see animals at Serengeti. When they reached Arusha they met many tourists, and they went to Serengeti together. Tatu was very glad to get this opportunity to show her children this big plain for animals.

Although they were inside a car, Sijali was frightened when she saw a lion lying down and giraffes eating grass. Her mother said to her, "Don't be afraid, there is no danger." Mashaka and Chausiku had their own private talk. I don't know what they were talking about. I think they were talking about the wild animals. This was their first time to see so many animals.

They were very happy.

In the evening Tatu and her children returned to Arusha town and slept at their aunt's. Her children described what they had seen in Serengeti. Their aunt was very glad to hear their stories. Finally, she said, "I will also go to Serengeti next year when you go there, or what do you say?" The children answered all together, "Yes, aunt, let us go together, Serengeti is very nice. It is one of the wonders of the world, is it not mother?" Their mother was in the bathroom ; she did not hear what her children had said. If she had heard, no doubt she would have agreed with her children.

EXERCISE 43 (Pg. 121)

1. What is Serengeti ? Where is it?
2. What do people go to Serengeti for?
3. Who was afraid of the lion at Serengeti ?
4. Where do the tourists who visit Serengeti come from ?
5. Where did Tatu meet the tourists ?
6. Who said, "There is no danger?" Why did she say so?
7. Where did Tatu and her children sleep when they came from Serengeti?
8. What did their aunt say?
9. Who said Serengeti is one of the wonders of the world?
10. Who was in the bathroom?

LESSON 36

THE AIRPORT

Tatu had a friend called Wambura. One day, Wambura wrote Tatu a letter. In the letter she said, "Hallo my friend, I will come by plane the day after tomorrow, we shall meet and talk about many things... "Tatu went to the airport to receive her friend. Wambura came from Nairobi by the morning plane; they left Nairobi at 8 a.m. and arrived at Arusha at 8.30 a.m. When the plane landed, Wambura came out with other passengers. Tatu took her luggage and put it in a taxi. On the way they talked happily, laughing heartily now and then. The taxi driver was also happy to listen to their talk. It is indeed a great joy to see people who love one another.

When they reached Tatu's home, the children came out to greet the guest. Mashaka helped to carry the luggage and Chausiku laid the table. Sijali was playing outside with her companions. Her mother called her and she came at once. In the evening Wambura told them about her flight.

EXERCISE 44 (Pg. 127)

1. Who is Tatu's friend? Where does she live?
2. From whom was the letter? What did it say?
3. When did Tatu's friend arrive at Arusha?
4. How long did the plane take from Nairobi to Arusha?
5. Why was the taxi driver happy?
6. Where was Sijali when her mother called her?
7. Who helped to carry the luggage?
8. What did Chausiku do?
9. Who travelled by air and later on talked about it?
10. What did Wambura do when the plane landed?

A STORY

A plane was in the air. The pilot told the passengers, "You may smoke now." After a little while he shouted, "Put out your cigarettes quickly and put on your safety belts at once." All the people were frightened. The plane was above the clouds, it began to descend faster and faster. Under the clouds there was fog; the pilot could not see the airport. He tried to go round but the plane continued to descend. Finally, he landed on a field. This pilot was very skilled. Although the plane was out of order, he landed safely; nobody was hurt. When the plane had landed the passengers came out trembling. They all shook hands with the pilot and congratulated him for his bravery. Many people came to see the plane accident. They were surprised to see that all the passengers were safe. After an hour or so a helicopter came and took all the passengers away.

EXERCISE 45 (Pg. 130)

1. Why was the pilot congratulated by the passengers?
2. Where did the plane land? Why?
3. Who was hurt in that plane?
4. Why were the people surprised?
5. Who came to take the passengers away?

LESSON 37

AT WORK

Tatu has a big field. She works in the field with her children. Every year they plant good seeds of maize, rice, beans, and cassava. Tatu does not like a lazy child. One day, Mashaka came late to the field. His mother told him, "If you come late again you will cultivate alone when we go home". From that day Mashaka has not come late again to work. Tatu's children know that everyday must work. Tatu works hard, and her children also work hard.

Last year, Tatu and her children got a very good harvest. Tatu has no food problem, her children eat nutritious food everyday. Sometimes Tatu goes to the market to buy fish, onions, and meat. Everyday she gives food to her children to take to school. They help her with shamba work when they return from school in the evening. Mashaka works hard at school; his teachers like him very much. Chausiku has just begun attending school. Sijali is still small.

EXERCISE 46 (Pg. 132)

1. Who was late one day to report to work? What did Tatu say?
2. What has Tatu? With whom does she work?
3. Who got a good harvest last year?
4. Is there any food problem at Tatu's? Why?
5. What do Tatu's children take when they go to school ?
6. What do Tatu's children do when they return from school ?
7. Why is Mashaka liked by his teachers?
8. Does Sijali go to school ? Why?
9. When did Chausiku begin going to school ?
10. Who works hard ?

A POEM IN PRAISE OF WORK

1. Don't go to town to look for a job
   You will waste your time, that is clear
   Agriculture is the mainstay
   Of good life even in dry season.

2. If you want good food (you get it) in the field
   Fruits, eggs, there is their home
   In the morning you have tea with eggs
   At noon meat with potatoes and rice in the evening.

3. Human dignity, good life and neighbourliness

Are well established there without any mishap
You will never live alone, never
Relatives, neighbours, you live together happily.

4. In the towns people lack neighbourliness
The clerk does not know the messenger
They don't greet each other on the way
As they rush to work.

5. Money reigns in their innermost heart
When they don't get it they are not happy
They don't sleep when they lie down to bed
They would go even to the factories
(looking for a job to get money).

6. And you, take the advice, stay at home in the rural area
Build your house of worth (a worthwhile house)
You will get a child whom you will call Shabani
And lead a good life in your own home.

LESSON 38

OUR SCHOOL

Our school is in the village. Our village has many people and many of them have children. In our village every child goes to school. Our school has many boys and girls, but the boys are more than the girls. There are 260 girls, and boys are twice as many. How many boys are there? No doubt there are 520 boys. The total number of our school children is 780.

There are also many teachers, women and men. Male teachers are three times the number of female teachers. My sister is a teacher in our school. She was the headteacher last year. She refused to be the headteacher this year; she says that it is too much work, she does not get time to look after her children at home. Many people think that it is better that only men become headteachers, because they have more time than women, especially women who have small children.

The headteacher of our school is hard-working. All the children and teachers like him. One day, he told all the children to bring stones for building the standard seven classroom. The children brought many stones.

The headteacher also brought stones every moming. The children piled up their stones. Later they lined up and the headteacher inspected them to see if their hair, hands, feet and clothes were clean. The dirty ones were punished.

Few children go to secondary school from our school each year. We have only three children who are studying at the University of Dar es Salaam, and five at the Morogoro College of Education, near Dar es Salaam. Our teachers work hard in their difficult task of teaching our children different subjects.

In front of the school there is a big field which is cultivated by teachers and pupils. They plant various seeds every year and they get good harvests. Our school has no shortage of money for buying school equipment with. We, the parents, also help with the work in the school field. There is good cooperation between the school and the village.

EXERCISE 47 (Pg. 137)

1. How many girls has our school?
2. Who was the headteacher last year?
3. Who do many people think should be the headteacher? Why?
4. Why is it difficult for women to be headeachers?
5. Why do the children bring stones?
6. Why do the pupils stand in a line in front of the school everyday?
7. What happens to the dirty pupil?
8. How many children from our school are studying at the University of Dar es Salaam?
9. Why is it that our school has no shortage of funds for buying school materials?
10. What kind of relationship exists between the school and our village?

MAZUNGUMZO

(Tatu azungumza na mtoto wake, Mashaka)

Tatu Was the examination difficult?

Mashaka Yes, the examination was very difficult.

Tatu Do you think you will pass?

Mashaka I don't know, but I did almost all the questions.

Tatu Did all the children find the examination difficult?

Mashaka Yes, every child said this examination was very difficult.

Tatu	What did your teacher say about this examination?
Mashaka	He did not say anything. He only said, "Take it easy children!"
Tatu	When will the results be out?
Mashaka	The results will be out next month.
Tatu	If you pass where will you go?
Mashaka	If I pass, mother, I will go to secondary school.
Tatu	What do you want to study for? What profession do you like?
Mashaka	I want to be a doctor and treat patients. Our country has not got enough doctors, and patients are very many.
Tatu	That is very nice, my child, I will be very happy if you become a doctor.

LESSON 39

THE POLITICS OF TANZANIA

Tanganyika is a big country; it is in East Africa. Long ago Persians, Arabs, Indians and, later on, Europeans came to the east coast of Tanganyikas to trade.The Arabs took slaves, they engaged in slave trade. The Europeans brought colonialism and imperialism to Tanzania.

Tanganyika fought for their independence. Today Tanzania is a free country. The leaders always say, "Freedom and work!"

Everybody must work. The policy of Ujamaa (Socialism) and Self-Reliance stresses work.

All Tanzanians must work hard to develop their country. Tanzania has a population of more than forty million. It has many children and few old people; children are twice as many as the old people. All these children must go to school to be educated. Many schools have been built by the citizens.

The Tanzania ruling Revolutionary Party (CCM) believes in the equality of all men, and practises the policy of social equality, irrespective of race, religion, etc. All Tanzanians speak Swahili, their national language.

Tanzanians are hospitable people; if you come to Tanzania you will enjoy living with them. In order to enjoy your trip to Tanzania learn Swahili. Many visitors who come to Tanzania learn Swahili; Many of them say that Swahili is one of the easiest languages in the world. Make an effort to learn Swahili now. If you want to speak, good Swahili, come to Tanzania after finishing this book. When you get here speak Swahili every day without fear of making mistakes.

EXERCISE 48 (Pg. 142)

1. Where is Tanzania?
2. What did the Tanganyika fight for?
3. Why did the Arabs come to the (east) coast of Tanganyika?
4. What is the population of Tanzania?
5. Who built many schools in Tanzania?
6. What would you do in order to enjoy your trip to Tanzania?
7. Where would you go to learn good Swahili?

8. Is there any discrimination in Tanzania?
9. Why should all Tanzanians work hard?
10. Who came to Tanganyika to trade?
11. Who says, "Freedom and Work!"?
12. What would you do to l earn good Swahili when you come to Tanzania?

LESSON 40

TATU GOES TO THE POST OFFICE

Tatu went to the post office to post her letter to her friend, Wambura. Tatu lives in Tanzania and Wambura lives in Kenya. Tatu and Wambura often write each other letters. Every year Tatu and Wambura meet once either in Arusha or in Nairobi. Last year Wambura came to Arusha, this year Tatu is going to Nairobi? Before she departs (for Nairobi), Tatu must write Wambura a letter informing her the day and hour of her arrival.

Tatu got a letter from Wambura in Nairobi the day before yesterday. Tatu answered it at once. She said, "Dear Wambura, greetings. Thank you for your nice letter. I am glad to hear you had a safe trip (you arrived safely). "Pole" for the long trip. You are lucky, you travel by plane. I have never been on a plane. I always travel by bus or by train. If I get money, this year I will come to Nairobi by air. I will let you know early enough so that you come to meet me at the airport..."

These days many people write one another letters. Letters are carried by air, by train, by bus or on foot. Long ago messengers in England used to carry mail on horse-back; in Arabia they used camels; and here in our country, they went on foot.

EXERCISE 49 (Pg. 145)

1. Does Tatu work at the post office?
2. Why did Tatu go to the post office?
3. Where does Tatu's friend live? What is her name?
4. When did Tatu get a letter?
5. How are letters carried these days?
6. What did the Arab messengers ride formerly?
7. In which country did the messengers go on foot?
8. Who has not been on a plane yet, Tatu or her friend?
9. Where is Tatu going this year?
10. How often does Tatu meet her friend?

VOCABULARY

VOCABULARY

Only words used in the exercises are given here. It follows therefore that the words in the lists of useful phrases should be learnt and referred to as and where they appear. The English-Swahili vocabulary list has, therefore, been deliberately kept short.

In the Swahili-English section the plural prefixes of nouns are given after the stem. If no plural prefix appears it means that the noun either has no plural or does not change its form in the plural, e.g. *nyumba,* -house(s)-.Verbs have been listed by their stems i.e. without the prefix *ku-*, which is,

however, given immediately after the stem, e.g. *–enda, ku-*, to go: etc.

Some of the words given here have more meanings than the ones given. The author has given only the meaning appropriate to the text The student is thus advised to consult the *Swahili-English Standard Dictionary* for detailed definitions of the words.

SWAHILI-ENGLISH VOCABULARY (WORDS USED IN THE EXERCISES)

A

-a,	of (takes class prefixes)
a-,	he, she (used with verbs)
abiria	passenger
acha,ku- kuachana,	to stop doing something
adhuhuri,	midday
adui,	enemy
afisa,	officer
afisa tawala,	administrator
Afrika,	Africa
Afrika Mashariki,	East Afrika
Afrika Magharibi,	West Africa
aga, ku-,	to take leave of
agana, ku-	to agree upon something
ahadi,	promise
aina,	kind, sort
aina gani?	What kind, what sort…?
ajabu, maajabu	wonder(s)
ajali,	(1) accident (2) fate
akiba,	savings
-ako,	your (sing.)
akili,	intelligent

alama,	sign, mark
alfu,	thousand, (see *elfu*)
alika, ku-	to invite
amini, ku-	to trust, believe in
kuamkia, ku	to greet
kuamsha, ku	to awaken
ana,	he/she has
andaa, kuandika,	to prepare, set in order
anga, angani,	sky, in the sky
angalia, ku	to see,
angu,	my, mine
anguka, kuangusha,	to fall down
kuanza,	to begin, start
-ao,	their
ardhi,	land
ari,	eagerness
arifu, ku-	to inform
asante,	thank you, Thanks
asubuhi,	morning, in the morning
asubuhi sana,	very early in the morning.
Leo asubuhi,	this morning
au,	or

B

baada ya,	after
baadaye,	afterwards
baba,	father
babu,	grandfather
bado,	not yet, still
bado kidogo,	a little while, yet
bado mtoto,	(he/she) still a child
bahari,	ocean, sea
baharini,	in, at the ocean
bahasha,	envelope
bahati,	luck
baki, kubaki,	remainder, rest, to remain
bakshishi,	tip
banda,	hut
bandari,	port, harbour
barabara,	road
baraka,	blessing
baridi,	cold
barua,	letter
basi, mabasi,	bus(es)
-baya,	bad
beberu, ma	imperialist (lit. he-goat)
bendera,	flag
bepari, ma-,	capitalist
bia,	1) beer 2) share; partnership (in business)

biashara,	trade, business
bibi, ma-	grandmother, lady
-bichi,	unripe, uncooked
bidhaa,	goods, merchandise
bidii,	effort, with effort
bila,	without
bizari,	curry powder
blanketi,	blanket
boma,	headquarters, fort
bora,	excellent, very good
-bovu,	rotten, out of order
bunduki,	gun
bunge,	parliament
bure,	in vain, grati s
bustani,	garden
bwana, ma	- lord, master

CH

-chache,	few
-chafu,	dirty
chafuka, ku-	become dirty, be excited
chagua, ku-	to choose, to vote
chai,	tea
chakula, vy-	food
cheka, ku-	to laugh

chekelea, ku- (tabasamu)	to smile
chekesha, ku-	to amuse
chelewa, ku-	to be late
chemka, ku-	to boil
chemsha, ku-	to cause to boil
cheni,	chain
cheo,	rank, social status
cheti, vy-	certificate
cheza, ku-	to play
chini,	down, under
choka, ku	to be tired
chombo, vy	vessel (of any kind)
choo, vy-	toilet
chui,	leopard
chukua, ku-	to take
chuma, vy-	iron (metal)
chuma, ku-	to pick (fruits, vegetables, etc.)
chumba, vyu	room
chuo, vy-	college
chuo kikuu,	university
chupa,	bottle

D

dada,	sister
dakika,	minute
dalili,	symptom, mark (see *alama*)
damu,	blood

darasa,	classroom, class
dawa,	medicine
deki, ku-	to wash the floor
dereva, ma-	driver
desturi,	custom, routine
dini,	religion
dogo, n-	small, little
duka, ma-	shop
dunia, duniani,	world, in the world

E

-ekundu,	red
-elea, ku	to float
-elewa ku-	to understand
eleza, ku-	to explain
elfu,	1 ,000
elimu,	education
-ema	kind, good at heart
-embamba,	slender, slim
embe,	mango
enda, ku-	to go
endelea, ku-	to go on, to progress
(maendeleo)	(development)
endesha, ku-	to drive
-enu,	your (pl.)
-enye,	having

-enye nguvu,	strong
-enyewe,	self, (e.g. mimi mweyewe, I myself)
-epesi,	light (not heavy)
-eupe,	white
-eusi,	black
-etu,	our

F

fa, ku-	to die
faa, ku-	be useful , fit
fahamu, ku-	to know
fahari,	glory, splendour
faida,	profit
faidika, ku-	to profit
fanya, ku-	to do, make
fanyika, ku-	to be done
faraja,	comfort, consolation
farasi,	horse
faulu, ku-	to pass, to succeed
fedha,	money
ficha, ku-	to hide
fika, ku-	to arrive
fikiri, ku-	to think
fikiria, ku-	to think of, to consider
fimbo,	stick

fisi,	hyena
fomu,	form
fua, ku-	to wash clothes
fulia, ku-	to wash clothes for
fuata, ku-	to follow
fukuza, ku-	to chase, to drive away
fulani,	certain person
fundi, ma-	skilled worker
fundisha, ku-	to teach
funga, ku-	to tie up, to shut
funza, ku-	to teach (not so frequently used)
fupi,	short, shallow
furaha,	joy,
furaha ku-	to be happy

G

gani?	which? (kitu gani? mtu gani?)
gari, ma-	car
gawanya, ku-	divide
gazeti, ma-	newspaper
giza,	darkness
ghali,	expensive
godoro,	mattress
-gumu,	difficult

H

haba,	little amount
habari,	news
habari gani?	how are you?
hadithi,	story
hafifu,	of poor quality
haidhuru,	it does not matter
haki,	justice
hakika,	certainly
hakuna,	there is/are not
halafu,	afterwards
hamsini,	fifty
hapa,	here
hapana,	no, not so
hapo,	there, on the spot, there upon
haraka,	haste
haribika, ku-	to be broken, out of order
hasa,	especially
hasara,	loss
hasira,	anger
hata,	even
hata kidogo,	not at all
hatari,	danger
hawa,	these (people)
haya,	well, agreed
heko,	congratulation

heri,	happy state (*kwaheri*, goodbye)
hesabu,	arithmetic, calculation
hesabu, ku-	to count
hiki, hivi,	this, these (*ki/vi* class)
hivyo,	after that manner, so
hodi,	Swahili way of "knocking at the door"
hodari,	brave
hofu,	fear
hujambo?	how are you?
huko,	there
huyu,	this person
huzuni,	sorrow

I

iba, ku-	to steal
idara,	department
imara,	firm
ingia, ku-	to enter
-ingi,	much, many
-ingine,	other
ingiza, ku-	to cause to enter, put into
isha, ku-	be finished, complete
ishi, ku-	to live
ita, ku-	to call
iva, ku-	be ripe, cooked

J

ja, ku-	to come
jaa, ku-	be full
jambo	hello
jambo, mambo	matter(s)
jamaa,	family (from which *Ujamaa* is derived)
jamii,	society, community
jana,	yesterday
janja,	clever
japo,	although
jaribio, ma-	trial, experiment
jaribu, ku-	to try, attempt
je,	well (introducing a question) how? (suffixed to verb)
jenga, ku-	to build
jibu, ku-	to answer
jibu, ma-	answer(s)
jicho, macho,	eye
jifunza, ku-	to leam
jiko, meko	kitchen
jina, ma-	name
-jinga,	foolish
jino, meno,	tooth
jioni,	evening, in the evening,
jiwe, mawe,	stone

jogoo,	cock
jua,	sun
jua, ku-	to know
juhudi,	effort
julikana, ku-	to be known
jumla,	total number
jumlisha, ku-	to add up
juu ya,	on top of, concerning
juzi,	day before yesterday

K

kaa, ku-	to sit. dwell in a place
kaanga, ku-	to fry
kabisa,	utterly, exactly
kabla ya,	before
kadiri ya,	according to
kahawa,	coffee
kaka,	elder brother
kali,	sharp, fierce, severe
kama,	if, as
kamata, ku	to catch
kamili,	complete
karani,	clerk
karibisha, ku-	to welcome, receive
karibu!	welcome!
karibu na,	near

kasirika, ku	to be angry
kataa, ku-	to refuse
kata, ku-	to cut
kataza, ku-	to forbid
katikati ya,	in the middle of
katika,	in, inside
kati ya,	between
kavu,	dry
kawia, ku-	to delay
kelele,	noise
kesho,	tomorrow
kiasi,	measure, amount
kiasi gani?	how much?
kiatu, vi-	shoe
kiazi, vi-	potato
kiboko, vi-	hippo
kichwa, vi-	head
kidole, vi-	finger
kidogo,	a little
kidudu, vi-	insect
kifaru, vi-	rhino
kifua, vi-	chest
kijana, vi-	youth
kijiji, vi-	village
kijiko, vi-	spoon
kikapu, vi-	basket
kike,	female

kikohozi,	cough
kikombe, vi-	cup
kila,	every
kilimo,	agriculture
kilo,	kilogramme
kimbilia, ku-, kimbiza, ku-	run, to drive fast
kinywa,	mouth
kinywani,	in the mouth
kiongozi, vi-	leader
kioo, vi-	mirror, glass
kipofu, vi-	blind person
kisha,	thereafter
kisima, vi-	well (of water)
kisirani,	mishap, misfortune
kisiwa, vi-	island
kisu, vi-	knife
kitabu, vi-	book
kitanda, vi-	bed
kitendo, vi-	deed
kiti, vi-	chair
kitivo, vi-	faculty
kitu, vi-	thing
kitunguu, vi-	onion
kiu,	thirsty
kiwanda, vi-	factory
kiwanja, vi-	kiwanja
kiwete, vi-	lame person

kiziwi, vi-	deaf person
kondoo,	sheep
kosa, ma-	mistake, error
kosa, ku-	to miss, to error
kubali, ku	to agree
kubwa,	big, great
kucha, ma-	claw
kuhusu,	about, concerning
kuku,	hen
kule,	there
kuliko,	more than
kumi,	ten
kuna,	there is/are
kura, (piga)	vote, to vote
kuta, ku-	to find
kukutana,	to meet
kutwa,	all day long
-kuu,	big, chief, *chuo kikuu*, university
mwalimu mkuu,	headmaster
kwa,	to, for
kwa nini,	why?
kwa sababu,	because
kwama, ku	to get stuck
kwamba,	that, (conjunctive)
kwanza,	firstly
kwao,	to their, in their home country
kweli,	surely, indeed
kwenu,	at, to your home (country)
kwetu,	at, to our home (country)

L

la,	no, *la hasha*, not at all
la, ku-	to eat
ladha,	taste
laini,	soft
lainisha, kulainisha	to make soft
laki,	100,000
lala, ku-	to lie down, to sleep
lami,	tarmac, *barabara ya lami*, tarmac road
laza, ku-	to lay down. *Laza mtoto*, put child to sleep
lazima,	necessary. *Ni lazima*, it is necessary
lea, ku-	to bring up (children)
lemea, ku-	to weigh heavily upon, to press down
leo,	today
leseni,	license
leso,	handkerchief
leta, ku-	to bring
lewa, ku-	become drunk
lia, ku	to cry,weep
lima, ku	to till the land, to cultivate
limao, ma-	lemon
linda, ku-	to protect, to watch over
lisha, ku-	to feed

liwa, ku	to be eaten
lowa, ku	to become wet
lugha,	language
lulu,	pearl, precious stone

M

-m-,	him, her
-m-,	you (pl)
Maajabu,	wonders
maana,	meaning; *haina maana* it has no meaning, it is nonsense
maarifa,	experience, knowledge, subject matter
maarufu,	noted, famous
mabasi,	buses
maendeleo,	development
mafuta,	oil
mahali,	place
maharage,	beans
mahindi,	maize
maisha,	life
majani,	grass
maji,	water
mali,	wealth
maliza,	to finish

mama,	mother
mambo,	matters
mapema,	early
mapenzi,	love, affection
majira,	times
magonjwa,	sicknesses
mashariki,	east
matata,	troubles
mate,	saliva
matokeo,	results
mauti,	death
mavuno,	harvest
maziwa,	milk
mazungumzo,	talk, conversation
mbali,	far away
mbalimbali,	different
mbegu,	seed
mbele,	in front
mbili,	two
mbio,	running speed
mbizi,	dive, *piga mbizi* to dive
mboga	vegetable
mbona?	why then?
mbuga,	plain
mbuzi,	goat
mbwa,	dog
mchana,	day time

mchele,	rice (uncooked)
mchungaji,wa-	pastor
machungwa, mi	oranges – orange trees
meli,	meli
meza,	table
mfanyakazi,	worker
mfuko,	pocket, bag
mgambo,	proclamation (militia)
mganga, wa-	doctor
mgeni, wa-	guest, visitors
mgongo, mi-	back
mgonjwa,	sick person, patient
mguu, mi-	leg, foot
Mhindi, wa-	1. Indian 2. Maize plant (pl. mi-)
Mia,	hundred
milioni,	million
Mjerumani. (Mdachi),	Germany
mji, mi-	town, city
mjukuu, wa-	grandchild
mkanda, mi-	belt
mkate, mi-	bread
mke, wa-	wife
mkizi,	type of fish
mkono, mi-	hand, arm
mkulima,	farmer, peasant
mkurugenzi,	director
mlango,	door

mle,	in that place
mlevi, wa-	drunkard
mno,	too much
mnyama,	animal
moja,	one
moja kwa moja,	straight on
moja moja,	one by one
moshi,	smoke
moto,	fire
moyo,	heart
mpaka, mi-	limit, boundary
mpaka,	until
mpishi,	cook
msaada, mi-	help
msafara, mi-	caravan
msafiri, wa-	traveller
msichana, wa-	girl
msisimko,	awakening
msingi, mi-	foundation
mstari, mi-	line
mtalii, wa-	tourist
mtende, mi	palm tree
mti, mi-	tree
mtihani, mi-	examination
mito,	1. pillow 2. river
mtoto, wa-	child
mtu, wa-	man, person

mtumishi,	servant
muda,	period, duration
muhimu,	important
mume, wa-	husband
mvua,	rain
mvulana, wa-	boy
Mwaajemi, wa-	Persian
mwaka, mi-	year
mwalimu, wa-	teacher
mwalimu mkuu,	headmaster
mwana, wa-	one's own child
mwanadamu, wa-	human being
mwanafunzi, wa-	pupil. student
mwanamke, wa-	woman
mwanamume, wa-	man
mwandishi, wa-	writer
mwanzo, mi-	beginning
Mwarabu,	Arab
mwenzi, wenzi	companion
mwezi, mi-	month
mwongo, wa-	body
mwisho, mi-	end
mwishowe, mwishoni,	at the end
mwizi,wezi,	thief
mwongo, waongo,	liar
mzee, wa-	old man
mzigo, mi-	load, luggage
mizizi, mi-	root
Mzungu,	European

N

na,	and, with, by
-na-,	tense prefix (present tense affirmative)
nafasi,	space, opportunity
nami,	with me (so. nawe. with you. *naye, nasi, nanyi, nao)*
namna hii,	in this way; (*fanya namna hii.* do it in this way)
nanasi,	pineapple
nane,	eight
nanga,	anchor
nani,	who?
nawa, ku-	to wash face, feet and hands only
nawe,	with you
nazi,	coconut
nchi,	land
ndani,	inside
ndege,	1. bird 2. aircraft
ndivyo,	thus, that's how
ndizi,	banana(s)
nge,	scorpion
ndugu,	1.relative 2. comrade
nene,	fat (used of people; see *nono*)
nenepa, ku-	grow fat (of people)
neno, ma-	word

ngamia,	camel
-ngapi?	how many?
ngazi,	ladder, step
ngoja,	ku- to wait
ngojea,	ku- to wait for
ngoma,	drum, dance
ng'ombe,	cow, cattle
nguo,	clothes, dress
ngurumo,	thunder
nguruwe,	pig
nguvu,	strength, force
ni,	is, are
ni-,	I (affixed to verbs)
nini?	what?
njaa,	hunger
nje, (ya)	outside
njia, njiani,	way, on the way
njoo, njooni,	come
nne,	four
mafuta,	fat (of animal)
nunua,ku-	buy
nusu,	half
nyama,	meat
nyamaza,	to keep quiet
nyani,	monkey
nyati,	buffalo
nyesha, ku-	to rain
nyoka,	snake
nyoya, ma-	feather

nyuki,	bee
nyuma (ya),	behind
nyumba,	house(s)
nyuso,	faces (sing. *uso*)
nywa, ku-	drink
nywele,	hair
nzige,	locust

O

oga, ku-	to marry (refers to a man)
olewa, ku-	marry (refers to a woman)
oa, ku-	to take a bath
ogelea, ku-	to swim
ogopa, ku-	- to fear
omba, ku-	to beg, ask for something
ona, ku-	to see
ondoa, ku-	to remove
ondoka, ku-	to depart
onekana, ku-	to be seen, be visible
ongea, ku-	to speak
ongeza, ku-	to increase, add to
onyesha, ku-	to show
-ote,	all
ote,	any
oza, ku-	1. to rot 2. to give in marriage

P

pa, ku-	to give
pahali,	place
paka,	cat(s)
paka, ku	smear, *paka rangi,* to paint
pakia, ku-	to load
pakua, ku-	to unload
pale, pale pale	there, right there on the spot
palipo (na)	where there is
pamoja,	together
pana,	wide
panda,	to plant
panda, ku-	to climb up, ascend; *pandisha,* to raise, cause to go
panga, ku-	to rent a room, pango, ma-
panga, ma	big knife
kupanga,	to arrange a room
pangusa, ku-	to wipe
panya,	rat(s)
papai,	pawpaw(s)
pasa,	oblige, (used impersonally, see impersonal verbs pg 52)
pasua, kupasua, ku-	to break, to tear
pata,ku-	to get
patana, ku-	to agree on, get along with
peke,	alone (used with possessive pron with *y* prfix *pekey angu,*

	I alone etc.)
peleka, ku-	to send
pembe,	horn(s), corner
pembeni,	in a corner, privately
penda,	to love, like
pi,	which
picha,	pictures
pia,	also
piga, ku-	to hit, beat (*piga ngoma, piga pasi, etc.)*
pigania,ku-	to fight doe (*mpigania uhuru),* freedom figher
pikia, ku-	to cook for
pili,	secondly
pilipili,	pepper
pima, ku-,	to mesure, to examine (medically)
pisha, ku-	to let it pass *(nipishe,* let me pass)
pita,	to pass,
pokea,	to receive
pokewa, ku-	to be received
polepole,	slowly
pole,	sorry
pombe,	alcoholic drink, local brew, beer
pona,	to recover, get better from illness
popote,	anywhere, everywhere
posta,	post office
poteza, ku-	to get lost

punda,	donkey
pundamilia,	zebra
pungua, ku-	to be less
pungua, ku-	to reduce
pwani,	coast, at the coast
-pya,	new

R

raha,	happiness
rais,	president
rafiki,	friend (sometimes pl. *marafiki)*
rahisi,	easy,cheap
ramani,	map
rangi,	colour
refu,	tall, high, long, deep
remba,	decorate
rembua, ku-	to disfigure
rubani,	pilot
rudi,	to comeback
rudia,	to repeat
rudisha,	to give back
ruhusa, ku-	to permit
ruka, ku	to jump, to fly
rutuba,	fertility

S

saa,	time, hour, watch
saa ngapi?	what time is it?
saba, sabini	seven, seventy
sababu, kwa	reason,because
sadiki, ku-	to believe
safari,	trip, journey
safiri,ku-	to travel
safisha, ku-	to clean
sahau, ku-	to forget
sahihi,	correct
saidia, ku-	to help
salama,	safe, safely (*usalama,* safety)
salamu,	greetings
samaki,	fish
samehe, ku-	to forgive
sana,	very, very much
sanduku, ma-	box luggage
sasa, sasa hivi,	now, just now
sauti,	voice
sauti kubwa,	loud voice
sauti ndogo,	low voice
sawa, sawasawa,	equal, evenly, equally, all right
sehemu,	part, section
sema, ku-	to say
shababa,	aim, target

shahada,	degree,
shaka,	doubt(s)
shamba, ma-	field(s)
shangaa,	to wonder
shanga,	beads
shangazi,	aunt
shauri,	case, problem,advice, counsel
shida,	problem; (*ni shida*, it is a problem
shika, ku-	to catch, hold
shikamoo,	greetings to elder persons
shimo, ma-	pit hole
shinda, ku-	1. to overcome 2. to stay long somewhere
shindwa, ku-	to be beaten, be overcome, fail
shuka, ku-	to descend
shusha, ku-	to lower down, make descent
shule,	schools(s)
si,	is not, are not
siagi,	butter
siasa,	politics
sifa,	praise, prestige
sifu, ku-	to praise
sigara,	cigarette(s)
sijambo,	I am well
sikia, ku-	to hear
sikiliza, ku-	to listen
sikio, ma-	ear(s)

siku,	day(s)
siku hizi,	these days , nowadays
siku zote,	always
simama, ku-	to stand up, stop moving
simamia ku-	to supervise
simulia, ku-	to narrate
samba,	lion(s)
sina,	I have not
sindikiza, ku	to escont accompany
siri, kwa siri,	secret, secretly
sisi, nasi,	we, with us
sisi wenyewe,	we ourselves
sita,	six
sitini,	sixty
sivyo, au sivyo?	not so, it is not so?
siyo, siyo tu,	so, not only
sogea, ku-	to draw nearer
soko, sokoni,	market, at the market
soma, ku-	to read, reading
somea, ku-	to study for, to read to, for
starehe, ku-	1. comfort, ease 2. used in answer to *karibu kiti* (meaning I am comfortable)
subira,	patience
subiri, ku-	to wait for (patiently)
sukari,	sugar

T

taa,	lamp(s)
taasisi,	institute
tafuta, ku-	to look for
taifa, ma-	nation(s)
taja, ku-	to mention
tajiri, ma-	rich man
taka, ku-	to want, wish
takataka,	rubbish, filth, dirty
tambua, ku-	to recognize, realize
tamka, ku-	pronounce
tamko, ma-	pronunciation
tandika, ku-	to lay out, to set in order
tandika kitanda,	make the bed
tangu,	since
tangulia, ku-	to go before
tano,	five
tarishi, ma-	messenger
tatu,	three
tawala, ku-	to rule
tayari,	ready
tazama, ku-	to look at, to examine (immediately)
tele, vitu tele,	plenty, a lot of things
tembea, ku-	to walk
tembeza, ku-	to advertise, to show around
tembo,	elephant(s)

tena, sema tena,	again, say it again
tengeneza, ku-	to make, to repair
tetemeka, ku-	to tremble
thamani,	worth, value
thelathini,	thirty
themanini,	eighty
thumni,	50 cents
tia, ku-	to put in, to cause to enter
timiza, ku-	to fulfill, complete
tisa, tisini,	nine, ninety
toa, ku-	to give, to subcontract
tofauti,	difference
toka,	to come out from
tokea, ku-	to appear
tope, ma-	mud
tosha, ku-	to be enough
tosheleza,	to satisfy
tua, ku-	to land
tukuza, ku-	to honour, glorify
tuma, ku-	to send
tumaini, ku-	to hope for
tumia, ku-	to use
tumikia, ku-	to serve
tunda, ma-	fruit(s)
tunza, ku-	to care for
tu,	only
twiga,	giraffe(s)

U

u-,	you (sing.)
ua, ma-	flower(s)
ua, nyua,	courtyard, compound
Uarabuni,	in Arabia
ubaba,	fatherhood
ubaguzi	discrimination
ubao, mbao,	timber
ubavu, mbavu,	rib(s)
ubaya,	wickedness
ubeberu,	imperialism
ubaguzi,	election
uchunguzi,	investigation
udevu, ndevu,	beard
udogo,	smallness
udongo,	earth, soil
uenezaji,	spreading
ufagio, fagio,	broom(s)
ushindi,	success
ufundi,	skill, know how
ufupi,	brevity
ugonjwa, ma-	disease(s)
ugomvi, ma	quarrel(s)
ubodari,	bravery, skill
uhuru,	freedom
Uingereza,	England

ujanja,	cleverness, cunning
Ujerumani,	Germany
ujenzi,	building
ujinga,	folly, ignorance
ujirani,	neighbourhood
ukoloni,	colonialism
ukubwa,	greatness,size
ukungu,	fog
ukuta, kuta,	wall(s)
Ulaya,	Euurope
ulevi,	drunkardness
ulimwengu	universe
uliza, ku-	to ask, enquire
nyuma,	fork(s)
uma, ku-	1. To bite 2. To give pain
umeme,	electricity
umia,	to get hurt
umiza, ku-	to hurt, injure
umoja	unity
umri,	age
unga,	flour
uongo,	lie
upate,	so that you may get (special form of subjunctive)
upepo, pepo,	wind(s)
upesi,	quickly
urefu,	length, height, depth

usawa,	equality
ushanga,	bead
ushirikiano,	co operation
usiku,	night, at night
usiku wa manane,	dead hours
usingizi,	sleep (*yuko usingizini*, he is fast asleep)
uso, nyuso	face(s)
utalii,	tourism (*mtalii*, wa- tourist)
utelezi,	slippery (*kuteleza*, to slip)
utoto,	childhood
utu,	human, dignity
utumwa,	slavery (*utumwani,* in slavery;)
uzee,	old age; *mzee, wa-*, old man
uzi, nyuzi,	thread(s)
uzuri,	beauty

V

vaa, ku-	to wear (clothes)
valisha, ku-	to dress someone (*vika* is more common)
vibaya,	badly, wickedly
vivyo hivyo,	in the like manner, likewise
vizuri,	wcll, wcll donc!
vua, ku-	to undress

vuna, ku-	to harvest (*mavuno*, harvest)
vunja, ku-	to break something
vunjika, ku-	to break, be broken
vuma, ku-	be well known, notorious
vuta, ku-	1. to pull 2. to smoke

W

wa, ku-	to be
wahi, ku-	to be in time
wajibu,	duty
wakati, ny-	time
wala,	nor
wale,	those
wali,	rice (cooked)
wao,	they
wapi?	where?
washa, ku-	to light (fire, start a car etc...)
wavu, ny-	net (fishing)
wazi, wazi, wazi,	clear, open
waziri, ma-	minister(s)
weka, ku-	to put
wema,	kindness, goodness
wenzi,	companions (sing, *mwenzi*)
weza, ku-	to be able, can
wezekana, ku-	be possible

wezi,	thieves (sing)
wewe,	you (sing)
-wili,	two (e.g. *watu wawili,* two people)
wimbo,ny-	song(s)
wingu, ma-	cloud(s)
wino, wino,	ink, in ink
winda, ku-	to hunt
wizara,	ministry
wizi,	theft
woga,	fear

Y

yai, ma-	egg(s)
yeye,	he, she
yuko, wako,	he, she is present, they are present.
yupi,	which one (*mtu yupi?* which man?)

Z

zaa,	to bear (children), to be born
zaidi ya,	more than
zama,	to sink:
zamani,	formerly, in the past
zamisha,	to cause to sink

zawadi,	gift, present(s)
zidi, ku-	to do all the more, continue, increase
zima, ku-	to extinguish
zima,	whole, alive
zito,	heavy
zoea,	to be used to
zoezi,	exercise(s)
zuia, ku-	to prevent
zunguka,	to go round
nzuri,	nice, pretty

ENGLISH-SWAHILI VOCABULARY (WORDS USED IN THE EXERCISES)

A

again,	tena
age,	umri
agree,	kubali, ku-
also,	pia, vilevile
and,	na
answer,	jibu
axe,	shoka
at home,	nyumbani
at school,	shuleni

B

bad,	baya
banana,	ndizi
beautiful,	zuri
bed,	kitanda, vi-
better,	bora (kuliko, -zuri kuliko)
big,	kubwa
bit, a bit,	kidogo
body,	mwili
book,	kitabu

bother,	sumbua
bottle ,	chupa
box,	sanduku, ma
brave,	hodari
bread,	mkate
broad,	pana
bring,	leta, ku-
but,	lakini
by,	kwa, na

C

child,	mtoto, wa-
city,	jiji
clean,	safi
coconut,	nazi (pl) nazi
come,	ja, kuja
come back,	rudi, ku-
cook,	mpishi, wa- pika ku-
cover,	funika, ku-

D

day,	siku
day before yesterday,	juzi
day after tomorrow	keshokutwa
today,	leo

difficult,	gumu
disease,	ugonjwa, ma-
dress,	nguo
dog,	mbwa
door,	mlango

E

each, each other,	kila, na (attached to the end of the verb e.g. to like each other *kupendana*
ear,	sikio, ma-
easy,	rahisi
eat,	la, ku-
electricity,	umeme
every,	kila
everyday,	kila siku
everybody,	kila mtu
everywhere,	popote, kila pahali
eye,	jicho, macho
excellent,	bora
face,	uso, nyuso
few,	chache
field,	shamba. ma-
flour,	unga
flower,	ua, ma-
food,	chakula, vya-
forbid,	kataza, ku-
friend,	rafiki (*occassionaly pl* marafiki)

G

girl,	msichana, wa-
go,	enda, ku-
good,	zuri
goodbye,	kwaheri
grass,	majani
great,	kubwa
greet,	amkia
guest,	mgeni wa-

H

have,	kuwa na
has,	ana
hard,	gumu
hear,	sikia
here,	hapa
high,	refu
his,	-ake
home, at	nyumbani
hour,	saa
house,	nyumba
how?	-je? (suffixed to verbs)
how much,	kiasi gani?
how many,	- ngapi?
humanity,	utu
husband,	mume, wa

I

ill,	mgonjwa, wa-
important,	muhimu
it is,	ni
it is not,	si

J

joy,	furaha
just now,	sasa hivi

K

kind,	-ema
know,	jua, ku-

L

language,	lugha.
laugh,	cheka, ku-
learn,	jifunza, ku-
letter,	barua
light (n) ,	mwanga, -epesi
like,	penda, ku-, kama

little, -dogo; a little, kidogo
loaf, mkate, mi-
long, -refu
loss, hasara
love, penda, ku-

M

make, fanya, ku-
man, mtu, wa-
many, -ingi
matter, jambo, mambo
meat, nyama
milk, maziwa
money, fedha
morning, asubuhi ; *this morning,* leo asubuhi
mother, mama
mountain, mlima, mi-
must, lazima

N

name, jina, ma-
necessary, lazima
new, -pya
news, habari
nice, nzuri

O

old man,	mzee, wa-
often,	mara nyingi
or,	au
our,	-etu

P

patient,	mgonjwa
pencil,	kalamu
place,	pahali
play,	cheza, ku-
possible, it is	inawezekana
potato,	kiazi, vi-
profit,	faida

Q

quarrel,	gombana, ku-, ugomvi, ma
question,	swali
quickly,	upesi

R

rain(n),	mvua
rain(v),	nyesha, ku-
read, reading,	kusoma
river,	mto, mi-
room,	chumba, vy-

S

sad,	-enye, huzuni
sadness,	huzuni, uchungu
safe,	salama
safety,	usalama
salt,	chumvi
say,	sema, ku-
school, at-	shule , shuleni
see,	ona, ku-
separate,	tenga, ku-
shame,	haya
sharp,	kali
she,	yeye (mwanamke)
shop,	duka, ma-
short,	fupi
sick,	mgonjwa, wa-
simple,	rahisi
sing,	imba, ku-

song,	wimbo, nyimbo
stone,	jiwe, mawe
speak,	ongea, ku-
strong,	-enye nguvu
strength,	nguvu
sweet,	-tamu
swim,	ogelea, ku-

T

table, on the,	meza, mezani.
tall,	-refu.
tea,	chai
teacher,	mwalimu, wa-
teeth,	meno (see *tooth*)
than,	kuliko
theft,	wizi
thief,	mwizi. wezi
thing,	kitu, vi-
tomorrow,	kesho
too,	pia
too much,	mno
tooth, teeth,	jino, meno
town,	mji, mi-
trouble,	shida, taabu
two,	mbili

U

unity,	umoja
universe,	ulimwengu

V

various,	mbalimbali
very,	sana

W

wall,	ukuta, kuta
what?	nini?
when?	lini?
where?	wapi?
which?	-pi? gani?
why?	kwa nini?
want,	taka, ku-
water,	maji
way,	njia
who? whose?	nani? -a nani?
wife,	mke, wa-.
will (future),	-ta-
without,	bila

woman,	mwanamke,wanawake
wonder,	ajabu, maajabu
work,	kazi
world, in the	dunia, duniani
write,	andika

Y

yes,	ndiyo
yesterday,	jana
you,	wewe
youth,	ujana

Z

zeal,	bidii ; *with zeal* kwa bidii.

SWAHILI NOUNS ARRANGED ACCORDING TO THEIR NOMINAL PREFIXES

- WA CLASS

mchawi,	witchdoctor
mchungaji,	pastor, shepherd
mganga,	doctor
mgeni,	guest, stranger
mgonjwa,	sick person
mjinga,	fool
mjomba,	uncle (mother's brother)
mke,	wife
mkulima,	farmer, peasant
mlevi,	drunkard
mpishi,	cook
msimamizi,	supervisor, overseer
mtoto,	child
mtu,	man, person, human being
mtumishi,	servant
mtumwa,	slave
mume,	husband
mzee,	old man
Mzungu,	European

MW-WA CLASS

mwalimu,	teacher
mwana,	son, daughter
mwanafunzi,	pupil, student

mwanahewa,	airman
mwanamaji,	sailor
mwanasiasa,	politician
mwanamke,	woman (pl) wanawake
mwanamume,	man (pl) wanaume
Mwarabu,	Arab
mwananchi,	citizen
mwenyeji	1. Native 2. Host (pl) *wenyeji*
mwenzi,	companion (pl wenzi)
mwimbaji,	singer *pl* waimbaji
mwizi,	thief pl wezi
mwongo,	liar (pl waongo

M-MI CLASS

mchanga,	sand (pl michanga not used)
mche,	young plant, seedling
mchele,	rice (uncooked)
mchezo,	play, game
mchuzi,	gravy, sauce
mfereji,	drain, channel, canal
mfugo,	domestic animal
mfuko,	bag, pocket
mfupa,	bone
mguu,	leg, foot

NB Only irregular plural forms are given.

mji, town, city

mkasi,	scissors
mkate,	bread
mkeka,	mat
mkia,	tail
mkono,	hand, arm
mkuki,	spear
mkutano,	meeting
mlango,	door
mlima,	mountain

MW - WA CLASS

mzee,	old man
Mzungu,	European
mkutano,	meeting
mlango,	door
mlima,	mountain
mmea,	plant
moshi,	smoke
moto,	fire
moyo,	heart
mpaka,	1. frontier, boundary 2. until
mpango,	plan, arrangement
msaada,	help
mshahara,	salary
mshale,	arrow
msiba,	calamity
msikiti,	mosque

msingi,	foundation
mstari,	line
msitu,	forest
msumari,	nail
msumeno,	saw
mtaa,	section of a town, street
mtama,	millet
mtambo,	machine with spring action
mtego,	trap
mtelemko,	slope
mtihani,	examination
mti,	tree
mto,	1. river 2. pillow
mtumbwi,	dhow
mhogo,	cassava
mwaka,	year
mwanzo,	beginning
mwendo,	speed
mwezi,	month
mwiba,	thorn
mwisho,	end
mzinga,	beehive, cannon
mzigo,	load
mzizi,	root

MA CLASS

fungu,	heap, portion
gari,	car
gogo,	log
gugu,	weed
gunia,	sack, bag
gurudumu,	wheel
ini,	liver
jambo, (mambo),	matter, affair
jangwa,	desert
jani,	leaf
jembe,	hoe
jengo,	building
jeshi,	army
jibu,	answer
jicho (macho),	eye
jiko (meko),	kitchen
jina,	name
jino (meno),	tooth
jipu,	boil
jiwe (mawe),	stone
jogoo,	cock
joka,	huge snake
jongoo,	millipede
juha,	simpleton
juma,	week
jumba,	mansion

kaa,	coal, ember
karani,	clerk
kopo,	can
kosa,	error, mistake
koti,	coat
kovu,	scar
kundi,	flock, crowd
limau,	lemon
nanasi,	pinaple
neno,	word
papai,	pawpaw
pigano,	battle, fight
pigo,	blow, beat
pori,	wildness
sanduku,	box
shaka,	doubt
shamba,	field
sharti,	condition
shati,	shirt
shauri,	advice, counsel
shimo,	hole, pit
shina,	trunk, root
shoka,	axe
sikio,	ear
soko,	market
tajiri,	richman
tako,	buttock

tawi,	branch
tofali,	brick
tumbo,	stomach
tunda,	fruit
tundu,	hole
ua,	flower
wingu,	cloud
yai,	egg
zao,	crop
ziwa,	lake

NOUNS USED IN THE PLURAL ONLY

MA CLASS

maarifa,	experience, knowledge
maendeleo,	progress, development
mafuta,	oil
mahudhurio,	attendance
mahindi,	maize
maisha,	life, livelihood
maji,	water
majivu,	ushes
majonzi,	grief
malisho,	pasture
manukato,	perfume
manung'uniko,	grumbling
mapatano,	agreement
matata,	trouble

mate,	saliva
mateka,	prisoner(s) of war
mauti,	death
mavi,	excrement
mazao,	crops
maziwa,	milk
mazungumzo,	talk, conversation

THE KITU CLASS

kiasi,	measure
kiatu,	shoe
kiazi,	potato
kibanda,	shed; hut
kiberiti,	match-box
kiboko,	hippo; whip
kichaa,	madness
kichwa,	head
kidole,	finger
kidonge,	tablet, pill
kifaru,	rhino
kijana,	young man
kijiko,	spoon
kikapu,	basket
kiko,	smoking pipe
kikombe,	cup
kilimo,	agriculture
kinu,	mortar, mill
kinyozi,	barber
kioo,	glass, mirror

kipande,	piece
kipofu,	blind person
kiraka,	patch
kisahani,	saucer
kisiwa,	island
kisu,	knife
kitambaa,	cloth
kitabu,	book
kitanda,	bed
kitendo,	deed, action
kiti,	chair
kitu,	thing, matter
kitunguu,	onion
kivuli,	shade, shadow
kiwanda,	workshop
kiwanja,	plot (of ground)
kizibo,	stopper
kiziwi,	deaf person

When appearing before a vowel, It becomes *ch*, and vi becomes *vy:*

chakula (vyakula),	food
chama (vyama),	association, party
chandalua (vyandalua),	mosquito net
cheo (vyeo)	rank, social position
chombo (vyombo),	vessel (of any kind)
chongo,	one eyed person
chuma (vyuma),	iron
chumba (vyumba)	room,
chungu (vyungu),	earthenware pots

N CLASS

adabu,	manner
adhabu,	punishment
adui,	enemy
afya	health
ahadi,	promise
aibu,	shame
aina,	kind, sort
akiba,	savings
akili,	intelligence
alama,	mark, sign
amani,	peace
amri,	command
ardhi,	earth
asali,	honey
asili	origin
askari,	soldier
asubuhi,	morning
baba,	father
babu,	grandfather
bahari,	ocean
bahasha,	envelope
bahati,	luck
bakuli,	basin; bowl
bandari,	port
barabara,	road
barafu,	ice

baraka,	blessing
baridi,	cold
barua,	letter
bei,	price
bendera,	flag
biashara,	business
bidii,	effort
binti,	daughter
bunduki,	gun
chai,	tea
chapa,	1. print 2. brand
chemchemi,	spring (water)
chokaa,	whitewash, lime
chui,	leopard
chumvi,	salt
chupa,	bottle
dakika,	minute
damu,	blood
daraja,	bridge
dawa,	medicine
debe,	tin (container)
desturi,	custom
dhahabu,	gold
dhambi,	sin
dhamira,	conscience
dini,	religion
dunia,	world

elimu,	education
fadhili,	virture
faida,	profit
farasi,	horse
fedha,	money
fimbo,	walking stick
fisi,	hyena
fitina,	malicious intrigue
fujo,	confusion
fulani,	a certain person.
furaha,	joy; pleasure
gari,	car (also in MA/class)
gereza,	prison
giza,	darkness
habari,	news
hadithi,	story
haki,	justice
hali,	condition, "state"
haraka,	haste
harufu,	smell
hasara,	loss
hasira,	anger
hatari,	danger
hatua,	step
haya,	shame, shyness
hema,	tent
heri,	happiness

hesabu,	arithmetic; sum
heshima,	honour
hewa,	air
hisani,	kindness
hofu,	fear
huruma,	mercy
idadi,	number
inzi,	fly
jamaa,	relative
jana,	yesterday
jasho,	sweat
jinsi,	sort, kind
jioni,	evening
juzi,	day before yesterday
kahawa,	coffee
kaka,	elder brother
kalamu,	pen, pencil
kamba,	rope
karamu,	feast, banquet
karatasi,	paper
kazi,	work
kelele,	noise
kengele,	bell
kesho,	tomorrow
kiu,	thirst
kodi,	tax
kofia,	hat, cap

kufuli,	padlock
kuku,	hen, chicken
kutu,	rust
maana,	meaning
mali,	wealth
mama,	mother
mamba,	crocodile
mara,	times (X)
mashine,	machine
mashua,	dhow
maskini,	poor person
mbegu,	seed
mboga,	vegetable
mbu,	mosquito
mbwa,	dog
mchwa,	ant (usually white ant)
meli,	ship
meza,	table
milki,	kingdom
mvi,	gray hair
mvua,	rain
nafasi,	opportunity; space
namna,	sort; kind
nauli,	fare
nazi,	coconut
ncha,	point
nchi,	country

ndege,	1. bird 2. aircraft
ndimu,	lime (fruit)
ndizi,	banana
ndoo,	bucket
ndugu,	relative
ndui,	smallpox
ng'ambo,	yonder; overseas
ngano,	wheat
ngazi,	ladder
nge,	scorpion
ngoma,	drum ; dance
ng'ombe,	cow, cattle
ngozi,	skin
nguo,	clothes
ngurumo,	growl, roaring, thunder
nguruwe,	pig
nguvu,	strength
nguzo,	pillar
nia,	intention
njaa,	hunger, famine
njia,	way
njiani,	on the way
njia-panda,	crossroad
nta,	beeswax
nusu,	half
nyama,	meat
nyani,	monkey

nyika,	wilderness
nyoka,	snake
nyuki,	bee
nyuma,	behind
nyumba,	house
nyundo,	hammer
nzige,	locust
orodha,	list
paka,	cat
pamba,	cotton
panga,	matchet
panya,	rat
pasi,	past, iron (for smoothing clothes)
pembe,	1. horn 2. corner
pesa,	money
pete,	ring
picha,	picture
pikipiki	motor-cycle
pilipili,	pepper
pombe,	alcoholic drink
posho,	ration
pua,	nose
pumzi,	breath
punda,	donkey
pundamilia,	zebra
pwani,	coast, shore
radhi,	pardon

radi,	thunder
rafiki,	friend
raia,	citizen
ramani,	map
rangi,	colour
risasi,	bullet
robo,	quarter
roho,	soul
ruhusa,	permission
saa,	hour, watch; clock
sababu,	cause
sabuni,	soap
safari, trip,	voyage
sahani,	plate
sakafu,	floor
salamu,	greeting
samaki,	fish
sanduku,	box, case
sauti,	voice
sehemu,	section, part
senti,	cent
serikali,	government
shabaha,	aim
sheria,	law
shida,	problem
siafu,	brown ant
siagi,	butter

siasa,	politics
sifa,	praise, qualification
sigara,	cigarette
siku,	day
simba,	lion
simu,	telephone, telegram
siri,	secret
sukari,	sugar
sungura,	hare
suruali,	trousers
sululu,	pick-axe
supu,	soup
suti,	suit
swala,	gazelle
taa,	lamp
taabu,	trouble
tabia,	character
takataka,	rubbish, refuse
tai,	1. vulture 2. necktie
tarehe,	date
tembo,	elephant
tende,	date (fruit)
thamani	value
tofauti,	difference
tumbaku,	tobacco
tumbili,	monkey
tupa,	file (for metal)

twiga,	giraffe
vita,	war
wasaa,	opportunity
wiki,	week
zamu,	turn, shift
zawadi,	present

U CLASS

Nouns with plurals

ua (nyua),	compound, courtyard
ubao (mbao),	timber
ubavu (mbavu),	rib
ubawa (mbawa),	wing
udevu (ndevu) ,	beard
ufa (nyufa),	crack
ufagio (fagio),	broom
ufunguo (funguo),	key
ukucha (kucha),	finger-nail
ukuta (kuta),	wall
ulimi (ndimi),	tongue
uma (nyuma),	fork
upande (pande),	side
upepo (pepo),	wind
ushanga (shanga),	bead
uso (nyuso),	face
wembe(nyembe),	razor
wimbo (nyimbo),	song

Nouns used only in the singular

uangalifu,	carefulness; care
ubaya,	wickedness
uchache,	scarcity
uchaguzi,	election
uchawi,	witchcraft
uchumi,	economy
udhaifu,	weakness
udogo,	smallness
Ufaransa,	France
ufundi,	skill
ugali,	thick porridge
uhalifu,	lawlessness
uharibifu,	destruction
uhuru,	freedom
Uingereza,	England
uino (wino),	ink
ujamaa,	socialism
ujana,	youth
ujanja,	cunning
Ujerumani (Udachi),	Germany
uji,	gruel
ujinga,	folly, (ignorance)
ukali,	fierceness, severity
ukanda,	belt
ukoloni,	colonialism
ukubwa,	size; greatness
Ulaya,	Europe
ulevi,	drunkenness
ulimwengu,	universe
ulinzi,	defence, care

umoja,	unity
umri,	age
unga,	flour
Unguja,	Zanzibar
unyonge,	weakness
unyonyaji,	exploitation
uongo,	lie
uongozi,	leadership
upole,	gentleness
upya,	newness
urefu,	length, height, depth
usahaulifu,	forgetfulness
usawa,	equality
useremala,	carpentry
ushindi,	victory
usiku,	night, at night
usingizi,	sleep
utajiri,	wealth,riches
utamu,	sweetness
utii,	obedience
utoto,	childhood, childishness
utu,	human dignity
uvivu,	laziness
uzazi,	childbirth, fertility
uzee,	old age
uzuri,	beauty

PA CLASS

pahali,	place(s) e.g. pahali pengi, many places
mahali,	place(s)

www.ingramcontent.com/pod-product-compliance
Lightning Source LLC
LaVergne TN
LVHW010319220926
848484LV00004BB/800
* 9 7 8 9 9 8 7 0 8 5 0 3 3 *